ORION PLAIN AND SIMPLE

meditation

LYNNE LAUREN

To my beautiful girls Kaeleigh and Stevie
and all our children of tomorrow

Copyright © Lynne Lauren 2010, 2017

The right of Lynne Lauren to be identified as
the author of this work has been asserted in accordance with the
Copyright, Designs and Patents Act 1988.

Previously published in 2010 as *Simply Meditation* by Sterling Publishing Co.,
Inc., New York

This edition first published in Great Britain in 2017 by
Orion
an imprint of the Orion Publishing Group Ltd
Carmelite House, 50 Victoria Embankment,
London, EC4Y 0DZ
An Hachette UK Company

1 3 5 7 9 10 8 6 4 2

Interior design by Kathryn Sky-Peck

A CIP catalogue record for this book is available
from the British Library.

Note: Every effort has been made to ensure that the information in the
book is accurate. The information in this book may not be applicable in
each individual case so it is advised that professional medical advice is
obtained for specific health matters and before changing any medication
or dosage. Neither the publisher nor author accepts any legal responsibility
for any personal injury or other damage or loss arising from the use of the
information in this book. In addition if you are concerned about your diet
or exercise regime and wish to change them, you should consult a health
practitioner first.

Paperback ISBN: 978 1 4091 6995 6

eBook ISBN: 978 1 4091 6996 3

Printed and bound by CPI Group (UK), Ltd, Croydon, CR0 4YY

www.orionbooks.co.uk

Contents

Introduction

Incorporating meditation into your life will help you feel happier and more at ease with yourself. It will aid you in coping with life and help you understand its twists and turns. It will also assist you as you try to relax. If your blood pressure is high, meditation can help you lower it. Meditation can also facilitate your contact with the spiritual realms.

In short, regular meditation can support you as you try to handle your life more effectively.

Once you have tried out some of the meditations in this book, you may wish to join others who meditate, or you may wish to take training in certain types of meditation; there are schools that focus on the techniques of zazen, vipassana, mindfulness, and yoga—just to name a few. With the rapid spread of meditation in the Western world, organizations and meditation centers have opened up in many towns and major cities.

If you are interested in any of the specialized types of meditation, contact your local Buddhist, Kabbalist, Zen, or spiritualist center to get further information on where to go to study further. Many forms of meditation follow religious beliefs (such as a Christian meditation group), and some do not, such as yoga classes. You will need to determine what appeals to you before following any one route.

This plain and simple book will introduce you to the main types of meditation: Buddhist, Zen, Taoist, and Transcendental Meditation. Most of the meditations are presented in this book in terms of their healing benefit, whether that healing benefit is physical, emotional, pyschical, or spiritual. You may see meditation as simply a means of relaxation, but it is so much more. Even the simple desire to become more relaxed will eventually lead to healing on multiple levels.

I have organized this book into three sections: the first part will prepare you for meditation and introduce you to the three Key Meditations from which all other meditations follow. Part two focuses on many forms of healing meditation—meditations that address emotional as well as physical distress. Part three presents more advanced concepts of meditation, which are meant to heighten your spiritual connections.

Although meditation can address emotional distress and aid in physical ailments such as high blood pressure, the meditations in this book do not—and should not—replace any medical treatment or advice you are receiving from a medical professional.

Part One

ABOUT
MEDITATION

What is
Meditation?

1

Meditation is a practice that calms the mind and body in a natural way. Its aim is to quiet or still your mind, which in turn will lead to calm awareness, without the interference of thoughts.

You can practice meditation at your own pace in your own time. No matter how infrequently you meditate, it will still have a beneficial effect, and the more you practice the easier it becomes.

Although meditation is relaxing, it should not be mistaken for a method of relaxation, because you must relax first in order to meditate. You don't put yourself into a sleepy daydream or far away state of mind, and you do not simply make your mind a blank. Meditation is a discipline that clears your mind and controls your thoughts and emotions so that you can function as your true self. You are not in a hypnotic state, because you are fully aware of what is happening here and now. Normally in life we put a lot of energy into thinking up ways of doing things or of achieving things, but as we begin to practice meditation, we break free and do the opposite to how we usually operate. Our energy is focused not on *doing* but on *being*, on ourselves, and on getting back to our real selves or our true nature.

Meditation techniques can range from chants and gentle breathing exercises, emptying the mind, focusing on one topic (single-point meditation) one movement or one of the five senses, to deep contemplation. In the East meditation is a central part of various religions and has been practiced for over 5,000 years to promote tranquility, awareness, and wisdom. Some of the methods are incorporated in the following practices.

Buddhist Meditation

Buddhist meditation involves a variety of techniques, including breath control and focusing on your mind (being aware of your thoughts, actions, and the here and now). Another meditation technique centers on visualizations or putting pictures in your mind—in other words, "seeing" a place, person, or situation in your mind's eye. These techniques are designed to develop your mind, improve concentration, and provide insight, peace, and tranquility.

Taoist Meditation

Taoist meditation has no religious background but is a way of *being* that works through meditation. The body is regarded as a sacred, and it is used to charge the body's natural energy into a force known as chi. This energy is then circulated internally. When the chi is flowing in your body and in the environment, you feel balanced with your true self, calm, and energized. Once you find your chi, the chi can be focused toward improving yourself or toward attaining goals in life. It is believed that once you attain chi, you need to put very little effort into life because it falls into place easily.

Transcendental Meditation

Maharishi Mahesh Yogi founded Transcendental Meditation, a mantra-based form of meditation, in 1958. Mantras are words, phrases, or sentences that when repeated have a power and energy that can have a positive effect on the person who says them. Essentially, this practice involves sitting with closed eyes, twice a day, for fifteen or twenty minutes at a time, while mentally repeating a mantra. The long-term aims are to move beyond the first three major states of consciousness—waking, dreaming, and deep, dreamless sleep—into the fourth state, the state of transcendental consciousness. With this technique your body and mind can gain deep relief from both mental and physical stress.

Zen Meditation

Zen meditation is a form of Buddhist meditation that simply means, "seated meditation." A type of Zen meditation is *Zazen*, which means "just sitting." This form of practice is highly personal; it is designed so that you seek enlightenment by focusing on the question, "What is life?" It also includes other forms of meditation such as stilling the mind, which stops you from thinking about day-to-day problems for a while. This involves the use of *koans*, which are stories, questions, or statements that go beyond rational understanding and activate the intuition. For instance, if you clap with two hands, there is a sound, and from this understanding comes the very famous koan: "What is the sound of one hand clapping?"

Why Meditate?

Meditation can help you to focus, de-stress, lift a low mood, heal, let go, improve your intuition, and keep your life in balance. It's the only way of feeling permanently calm and tranquil that has been available to us up until now. Other ways of calming, such as drugs and alcohol, only produce temporary escape and relief.

Who you are and how your life flows begin with your mind. You create your world, and your mind is the workshop where it all begins. You choose who you want to be, who is in your life, and how you deal with them. You choose what work you do, where you live, how you look. You are the only person in control in your life, and others cannot really make you do anything unless you agree to let them. When you are truly happy, you do not think and your mind is calm. If you feel you aren't good enough, or that good things will never come to you, then they never will, because you will never allow them to. Fears and phobias, or ideas such as believing that you can't live without something, or that what you want is always going to be out of your reach, are the inventions of your own mind. In reality, there is little outside of you that is stopping you from living and being who you really want to be. Meditation is a way of working on the mind in an unfolding and gentle manner, allowing you to realize, understand, and undo whatever is restricting you or making you unhappy. It also allows you to get to know your real self and to make changes that can help you communicate and handle life more easily. It can help you deal with, and rise above, the pressures of everyday living.

Research into the effects of regular meditation has found a wide range of benefits both mental and physical. Immediately noticeable is a drop in anxiety and tension and the relief of physical problems caused by stress and anxiety, such as palpitations, high blood pressure, headaches, insomnia, and even stammering. Meditation increases calm feelings, optimistic views, and feelings of self-worth. Meditation has been found to be good for those with creative minds—writers, artists, and musicians—as it can spark fresh ideas, and bring new insight and inspiration. This is particularly the case with visualization meditations. Those who feel stuck in life can sweep away the blocks and renew their motivation, efficiency, and energy by using meditation. Emotions can be calmed, healed, and lifted, often by just simply following the Buddhist breathing exercises.

Preparing Yourself for Meditation

2

As you progress in your practice of meditation, you will find you can do many of the simple exercises in a few minutes, anywhere, and anytime. You will get better at distancing yourself from your surroundings and turning your focus inward. The more you can bring meditation into your daily life, the more positive results you will see, and the calmer you will feel.

Where to Meditate

If you plan to meditate often or as a regular part of your daily routine, you'll find it useful to choose a quiet space with few distractions, where you feel happy, and where you can sit comfortably. It is especially good for your progress if the space you allocate is *only* used for meditation, since the space will accumulate a good vibration and become associated with the benefits of meditation. Good places could include an area of your bedroom or a living room. Keeping the meditation area simple will help prevent distractions. Many people find their meditation space to be more calming if the wall or surroundings are pastel colors such as lilac, blue, greens, or neutral colors such as cream or white. In the summer, you may feel like using a corner of the garden or perhaps a summerhouse, sunroom, sun deck, or conservatory. This is especially good if you want to use natural subjects as your source of meditation.

You will need something comfortable to sit on. An ordinary comfortable chair is fine; you may also use a hard high-backed chair with a cushion if you need to support your back. If you want to meditate in true Eastern style, sit cross-legged on a cushion.

Alternately, you can kneel and insert the cushion between your buttocks and your legs.

Your posture is important, especially when practicing Buddhist, Zen, and Taoist meditations because these are longer meditations and you will be sitting longer in one position. It is important to keep your back straight so that you stay comfortable. If you imagine there is an invisible thread pulling up the top of your head, straightening your back, this can be a comfortable posture to maintain

while doing any seated meditation. Your clothing should be comfortable and nonrestricting. Should you prefer to use incense, it is a good idea to use a stick that will roughly last the length of your meditation.

Meditate at the time of day that suits you best—for instance, during the morning, if that is when your mind is fresh. Some people are not morning people, and they prefer the quiet of evening as their meditation time. If you regularly wake in the wee early hours and find you can't get back to sleep, this is also a good time to meditate as it can focus and calm you. By setting a regular time slot for meditation, you will soon find that you look forward to it as a change from the normal stresses and activities of your lifestyle.

Putting Visualization to Work

Many of the meditations in this book are quick and effective, and you can even do some of them as you go about your daily life, say, while commuting on a train or bus, or while waiting in line. Needless to say, **never meditate while driving!** If you are sitting and worrying about something, try a meditation; you may find that it helps to relieve your worry.

Many of the meditations in this book are based on the technique of visualization, that is, creating pictures or images in your mind. You will "see" the person or problem with your mind's eye, and then use further images or pictures to solve or heal a problem. You will use your imagination and direct your own inner movie.

Visualizing in meditation works effectively on three aspects of our being: our physical bodies, our emotions, and our spiritual or soul level. Your body will believe the images that your mind focuses on, and here's why: your mind uses the images that your physical eyes see to enable you to live, so it will accept images that your inner eye shows it, and then your mind will tell your body how to act. (It's important here to mention that blind people can also practice visualization; their inner eye "sees" what their other senses perceive.) Just as your mind can tell you how to sit in a chair by gauging it's shape and size, so can your mind work on the healing of an organ in your body if you can see it becoming healed. Believe, and your body will respond.

The emotions are linked to the creative side of the brain, so they respond to music, poetry, art, and images. If you picture a beautiful desert island scene, you will feel your emotions reacting.

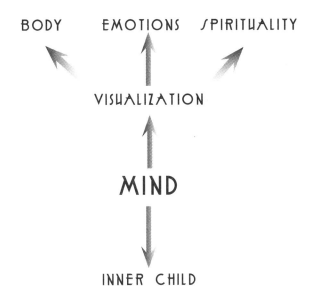

BODY   EMOTIONS   SPIRITUALITY

VISUALIZATION

MIND

INNER CHILD

When developing your psychic or spiritual skills, your imagination will trigger your third eye, the center that controls your psychic senses. For instance, if you look back into your past and the things that influenced you in your early days, you often can recall experiences as feelings and as pictures. We all have childhood memories, usually in the form of images in the part of our mind that still connects us to our childhood or our inner child.

Our minds have been shaped by our childhood memories, but when we are adults, our minds take in information from our eyes, as well as our other senses, and combined they create the window to the world around us. Our minds absorb all of this sensory stimulus, which then informs our visualizations, which in turn affects our bodies, emotions, and spirituality.

Preparatory Exercises

Many of the meditations in this book have short preparations or exercises to help you become calm and to focus your mind for the main meditation. These preparatory exercises are called the *Key Meditations* and you can use them whenever you feel it necessary to ground yourself or quiet your mind prior to beginning your main meditation.

Key Meditation One is good for calming your busy mind and focusing it properly, which is very helpful if you are the kind of person who tends to ruminate, or if you tend to run away with your thoughts. It will help still your mind. It is also a complete meditation in itself that you can use anywhere if you are stressed.

Key Meditation Two is a longer exercise that is used as a preparation for many psychic and spiritual meditations. It is good for clearing out any "heaviness" you may feel in your body, as heaviness is associated with darkness. Worry and upset can make us feel physically heavy. This meditation cleanses and relaxes your body and it also lifts your mood, allowing you to feel lighter and happier.

Key Meditation Three forms the framework that moves you toward deeper meditation and spiritual access. This meditation requires the use of your imagination, and this helps the development of your "third eye," which, in turn, helps improve your intuitive or psychic abilities. The third eye is also known as the brow chakra; it is located in the middle of the forehead between and a little above the eyes. This meditation will help you open this chakra to prepare you for any kind of psychic or spiritual activity.

Read through each meditation before following it. You may find it useful to record the instructions for the longer meditations, as this will allow you to relax and to get more out of them—until you have these meditations memorized, it can be awkward to keep referring back to this book for step-by-step instructions.

Key
Meditations

3

With these simple visualizations as starting points you can follow any of the meditations in this book more effectively, as they will allow your focus to be sharper and make the outcome stronger.

Key Meditation One: "Grounding"

You can do the "Grounding" meditation either standing or sitting. It is good for calming and bringing your focus into the present moment, the here and now. It is good for stress if your thoughts are whirling, or if you have just come away from an upsetting occurrence and your mind will not clear.

1. Relax and lower or close your eyes.

2. Focus on the arches of your feet.

3. Visualize two roots, one from each foot, growing down into the ground.

4. Allow the roots to work their way down, deeper and deeper.

5. Let the roots branch out as they go.

6. Feel yourself becoming calmer the deeper you take your roots.

7. Visualize your roots working their way further downward.

8. The roots pass through different layers of soil, clay, and rock.

9. Continue in this way until your feet begin to feel heavy.

10. Then bring your focus back up to your feet.

11. Lift or open your eyes.

Note: If you feel that you are not grounded enough you can add this following second step before opening your eyes.

Second Step

1. Take your focus to the base of your spine.

2. Imagine a thick root growing from the base of your spine.

3. See the root growing down through the chair (if you are sitting), then through the floor, and down into the ground.

4. Watch the root burrowing deeper and deeper.

5. Imagine the roots branching out into the earth.

6. The roots continue down through layers of soil, rock, and clay.

7. Feel your back firmly anchored to the chair.

8. Now bring your focus up to the base of your spine.

9. Lift or open your eyes.

Key Meditation Two: "White Light"

The "White Light" meditation is a good preparation for any psychic of spiritual meditation and also is an instant mood lightener. If we keep worrying about something, we can store this negative energy in certain parts of our bodies. This can make our bodies feel heavy, and eventually it can make us ill. When we are happy, our bodies feel light. This meditation cleans old suppressed hurts, anxieties, and upsets.

1. Sit quietly, relax, and close your eyes.

2. Take a few deep breaths, keeping your eyes closed.

3. Take your focus to the top of your head.

4. Send up a thought asking for a shaft of white light to come down from the Universe.

5. Visualize the light entering the crown of your head.

6. The light flows down into the top of your head, filling your crown.

7. The light flows down into your forehead, eyes, and temples.

8. It flows into your cheekbones, ears, mouth, chin, and jawbone.

9. The light completely fills the back and the front of your head.

10. The light flows down the length of your neck.

11. The light flows along the tops of each shoulder.

12. It flows down into both arms right to your fingertips.

13. Now take the light down through your chest, tummy, and abdomen.

14. Bring the light down both legs and into your feet.

15. When you are completely full of white light, drop it down into your feet, into the roots, and down into the earth.

Working with white light has a three-fold advantage. First, it lifts your vibration or the speed of your natural energy, which then lifts and brightens your mood and allows you to meditate more effectively. Second, it helps clear your system of negative energy that has gathered there from tension, stress, or emotional upset. Third, white light opens a clear communication channel that enables guides and the spirit world to contact you quickly and easily.

Key Meditation Three: "Spinning Disc"

The "Spinning Disc" meditation forms the framework for the work you will do on the mental, emotional, and spiritual aspects of yourself.

1. Find a quiet place you will not be disturbed.

2. Relax, close your eyes and take a few deep breaths.

3. Take your focus to your third eye and visualize a white spinning disc.

4. As you watch the disc, it grows larger and larger.

5. When the disc is large enough to step through, go through the center.

6. You will find yourself on an outdoor path on a bright sunny day.

7. The path leads you into a lovely garden.

8. The path meanders ahead.

9. The path leads you to the front door of a lovely house, your house.

10. You enter the house, closing the front door behind you.

11. You enter a beautiful hallway.

12. In front of you is a large stairway.

13. On the first landing there is a large window, casting pools of sunlight on the floor where you are standing.

14. There is also a stairway descending to a lower floor.

15. There are two corridors leading off to the left and right.

The meditations that use this Key Meditation will continue from this point by directing you to certain parts of the visualized house:

- The left-hand corridor is used for emotional meditations;
- The right-hand corridor is used for mental meditations;
- The stairway going up is used for spiritual developing meditations;
- The stairway down takes you into deeper strengthening meditations.

Part Two

HEALING
MEDITATION

Clearing
Negativity

4

The following meditations are designed to clear negative vibes that hold you back.

Clearing Stress

We suffer tension and stress on a daily basis, and unless we unwind properly and let these things go, they can build up in our system, affecting our moods making us lethargic and making our bodies feel heavy.

We absorb large amounts of negative vibrations from the world of gadgets we now live in, and these can also affect our physical and mental states. Computers, televisions, microwaves, and telephones all transmit energy that is lower than ours, and are therefore more negative than ours, and we absorb these into our system. Cars operate on a low vibration, which many people pick up on. Many people experience a change of mood as soon as they get into a car, especially when they get into the driver's seat. We see examples of this as sudden outbursts of impatience, and in extreme cases, even road rage. The same thing happens to some people when they get into an airplane.

The moods and actions of other people and our own negative reactions and worries also filter into our system and can be compounded as we play them over and over in our minds. Eating junk food or processed food that has very little natural goodness in it can upset our bodies, causing us to be fatigued and often irritable. If we eat the meat of animals that have been treated badly and who died in fear, those negative energies will transfer to us.

A daily clearing of the general negative energy in our systems help rid our systems of sluggish energy, calm our moods and be enormously energizing. Here are some simple meditations that can be fitted into your daily routine. They are quick and they will drain away any negative energy that you have. You can practice these while sitting at the office desk, standing at a bus stop, waiting in line or even while traveling.

This meditation can literally be done anywhere, even in company. It requires little focus and no visualization. You can effectively use it quickly in the middle of an interview, or in a meeting, or in any situation in which you have to deal with people. It is also useful if you find you are unable to unwind at the end of the day or if you are having trouble sleeping. This is best practiced while sitting.

1. On both hands, touch the end of your thumbs with your index fingers.

2. Spread open widely the other three fingers on both hands.

3. Rest the backs of your hands on your upper thighs.

4. Focus on your breathing and be aware of it becoming calmer.

5. Leave your hands in this position for as long as you need or want.

6. When you finish and release your fingers, allow your breathing to return to normal.

This meditation helps you slow down your breathing, which in turn will begin to de-stress your nervous system and calm your mind.

Clearing Negative Energies

These meditations help you draw away hurts, tensions, or upsets that have accumulated in the form of negative energy. This energy may have caused aches and pains. This exercise can be done standing or sitting, and anywhere at any time of the day. All you need is a minute or two of uninterrupted time; you will feel noticeably lighter immediately afterward. If you feel inclined you can take yours shoes off as this allows your energy field to expand, but this meditation will still work if you don't.

Opening Your Taps or Spouts

1.   Relax, take a few deep breaths, and close your eyes.

2.   Put your feet flat on the floor.

3.   Visualize your body from your feet to the top of your head and in your mind's eye, see it pure white.

4.   Look down at your feet.

5.   Notice any dark negative energy that has risen up your body.

6.   Is it ankle high, thigh high, waist high, or higher?

7.   Visualize two small taps, one in the sole of each foot.

8.   Open them to reveal two small drains, one on each foot.

9.   Push the negative energy out through these drains.

10. When all the negative energy has gone, close the shutters.

11. Open your eyes.

Wash Your Baggage Away

Negative energy in the form of low feelings, anger, or aggression can accumulate in our body's energy field or aura. This energy field is mainly the energy we give out; it surrounds our bodies and can extend up to several feet. When you are in water, your aura retracts into your body so that any negative energy in it just drops off.

This meditation is good to do in the bath or shower. It is a quick, inner cleansing and rejuvenating exercise while the water is cleansing your energy on the outside!

1. Close your eyes, visualize a white shaft of light.

2. Bring it down through the crown of your head,

3. Let it flow down through the inside of your body.

4. See the light washing away dark negative areas, negative feelings and tensions.

5. Let the light wash the dark energy down toward your feet.

6. Open two shutters in the soles of each foot.

7. See the negative energy drain out of your feet and down the drain.

8. Close the shutters and open your eyes.

The Sieve

This meditation is good when you're feeling overwhelmed with troubles and becoming despondent. It works by clearing your energy field around your body (the aura) as well as your energy system within your body.

1. Take a few deep, long out breaths and close your eyes.

2. Under your feet imagine a circular sieve with a fine golden mesh; it extends out four or five feet around your body.

3. Pull the sieve steadily up from the ground, up through your body and energy field.

4. Notice it catching and taking any negative energy up with it.

5. It moves up your whole body and through your head.

6. It stops above the top of your head.

7. Now see the outer edge of the sieve shrinking like elastic and pulling together to form a bag.

8. Imagine yourself taking the bag to a window and dropping it to the ground.

9. Alternatively watch it float upward until it diminishes into the distance.

10. Open your eyes.

If you find a room has a stale atmosphere you can "sieve" the room or a whole building by visualizing it moving upward through the room or building to the top.

Sieving on the Inside

This meditation is good after an upset or worry or whenever you feel as though you are carrying a weight inside your system. This can often be felt as a physical weight either in your tummy, abdomen or chest. You may find this best to do sitting or lying down. Give yourself at least five to ten minutes when first practicing.

1. Relax, take a few deep breaths, and close your eyes.

2. Visualize a golden sieve just below the base of your spine; see it as the same width and depth of your body.

3. Now visualize it has moved up under your spine *inside* your body.

4. Move the sieve upward internally, catching the heavy area.

5. Pull the edges of the sieve together around the heavy energy.

6. Pull it up through your body.

7. Take it out through the crown of your head.

8. Send it up and outward until it is a distant speck and diminishes.

9. When you are ready open your eyes.

Clearing
Past Hurts

5

Living in the past and replaying old hurts can hold you back, preventing you from achieving what you want in life, or from being the person who you want to be. You can get stuck in a rut and depressed as your feelings, thoughts, and body absorb the impact of long-term anger or upset. Illnesses can occur in the part of the body where the hurt has been stored; hanging on to heartbreak over a period of years can cause chest problems, or weaken the left hand side of your body.

Everybody has bad experiences and disappointments in life and letting go of bad memories or old issues is very important for your health, confidence, motivation, the way you function in the world, and the way you deal with other people. If you are holding onto an old hurt it can prove to be very damaging, not only mentally and emotionally but also physically and spiritually.

Removing Blocks

This meditation can take ten to fifteen minutes or longer, so it would be best to record it beforehand and then let the recording guide you through.

1. Find a quiet place you will not be disturbed.

2. Relax, close your eyes and take a few deep breaths.

3. Take your focus to your third eye and visualize a white spinning disc.

4. As you watch the disc grows larger and larger.

5. Step through the center.

6. You find yourself on a path on a bright sunny day.

7. The path is leading you through a lovely garden.

8. Visualize the plants and trees in detail.

9. You come across a spiral stairway, descending to a lower level.

10. Count yourself down the ten steps of the staircase.

11. Now you find yourself on a lighter path.

12. This is your time path.

13. It stretches both in front and behind you.

14. In front the path stretches forward disappearing into a distant horizon.

15. As you stand looking forward, your past should be behind you.

16. If you feel it is creeping around the sides or pulling you back, push it firmly behind you, then walk forward from it.

17. As you look forward, check if there are obstacles or people hindering your way.

18. If there are, remove them or let them fade away, then put them to the side of the path, or place them behind you until you can visualize your path as clear.

19. Now climb back up the ten steps.

20. Make your way through the garden.

21. Step back into the light of your third eye.

22. Blend back in with your body.

23. Align with your body so that you feel you are back in your feet, knees, elbows, and shoulders.

24. Wiggle your fingers and toes.

25. When you are ready, open your eyes.

Letting Go of Relationships

Sometimes we want to break away from a hurtful relationship but find we can't let go or that we keep being pulled back into it. Long after a separation or divorce we can still find that our "ex-partner" affects our feelings by upsetting us or by controlling us in some way. We can also feel affected if we allow a destructive friendship to continue when we really should bring it to an end.

What can happen is that the upset or anger you have felt with that person can accumulate and form cords of energy that stretch from their heart to yours. The same effect can occur from their throat to yours if you have exchanged hurtful words. There can be a cord linking you at the center of your tummies if there has been a power struggle between you. Ex-partners tend to be attached to the center of your abdomen from their abdomen or from third eye to third eye. The same can be said of a parent or teacher or anyone who has influenced you, as in this case, they can be attached from the crown of their heads to your crown or to the base of your spine.

If you have an uneasy feeling when you think of someone, there will usually be a negative connecting cord of some sort connecting you both. Cutting cords will not harm anything good between you and neither does it dispel them from your life—unless their reason for being in your life is purely negative. It removes negative influences that are still at work, such as bad thoughts or feelings left over from an argument, from bullying, or from a constant pattern of behavior, such as lying.

This simple meditation of cutting negative connections can free you to make the changes you need, or they will help you clear the air and sort things out positively.

Burning Negative Cords

This meditation can be quite effective last thing at night before you go to sleep, because your third eye is very receptive to images at this time. Also if you wake in the night and find yourself thinking of a person in a way that troubles you, try it then. You could notice a marked difference in what you feel or experience when you see them again.

1. Take a few deep breaths and close your eyes.

2. Visualize the person full length standing in front of you.

3. Check for cords connecting you to each other that run from their center to your center.

4. There may be only one or there may be many.

5. Focus on the lowest cord.

6. Visualize a colored flame and place the flame at your end of the cord.

7. Let the flame burn along the length of the cord.

8. Finish when the flame reaches the other person's center.

9. Leave no ends hanging.

10. Extinguish the flame and begin to work on the next cord, either using a fresh color for the flame or the same one.

11. Keep going until all cords are burned away.

12. Allow the person to leave your mind's eye.

13. When you are ready, open your eyes.

You may need to repeat this meditation two or three times before you see or feel a difference.

Removing Ties

This meditation can be very effective if you have had relationships where the responsibility has been loaded onto you. Maybe you were the one holding the household together, being the breadwinner, and paying the bills? Or you may have been emotionally supportive, providing companionship or keeping someone calm and protected from upsetting situations. You may have coped with someone with an addiction, depression, or an illness and they came to expect you to continue supporting them.

This meditation can help clear previous patterns of thoughts where a person expects you to be "doing" for them in some way.

1. Close your eyes and take your focus to your third eye.

2. Visualize the person in question standing behind you.

3. Scan for any connecting cords from the other person that are penetrating your back and shoulders.

4. Visualize a colored flame of your choice and begin burning all your cords.

5. Visualize the flame working back and burning all the cords to their starting points on the other person.

Note: Any color can be used for the flame—red, blue, green, white—choose the one that is most effective for you.

Freeing Yourself

You are a living being, and life creates energy and all around you your body there is an energy field called your *aura*. A special camera called a Kirlian camera can pick up this energy, and some people can see an aura with their physical eyes or with their inner eye or third eye. This energy can stretch out several feet from a person's body. Thoughts and feelings can show up as colors in your aura that can change from day to day or week to week.

Certain negative energies such as envy, jealousy, resentment, impatience, or anger, can be directed toward you from people you know or have known, or even those who you have briefly met. You may have felt this energy or you may have been upset by it afterward if you took it on board. It will have formed a restrictive layer closely around you, and it can show up as a dark area in your aura. This can make you feel vulnerable, fearful or anxious.

If some people have thought badly of you, whether you feel you have deserved it or not, or if you keep on attracting negative reactions from others, try the next meditation. If there is a negative band of energy around you, when you remove it you will feel a rush of fresh energy. This will flow from the base of your spine upward at the end of the meditation.

With practice you will find you can do this meditation anywhere and at any time in the space of a few moments.

1. Relax and lower or close your eyes, and take a few deep breaths.

2. Visualize the person in question full length in front of you.

3. Scan your head to see if a dark cap (like the old rubber swimming caps) is on your head.

4. Check how far it has stretched down your body.

5. It may cover your head, come down to your shoulders, and stretch over your chest or even cover your whole body.

6. Catch hold of the ends and roll it back up until you can lift it off your head.

7. Visualize a window, and send the cap out of the window, and let it drop into the ground outside.

8. Focus on the base of your spine.

9. Visualize yourself removing a plug from in front of your tailbone.

10. When your feel ready open your eyes.

Change
Your
World

6

This chapter helps you focus on those parts of your nature that you dislike—thoughts, feelings, and self-beliefs that you may be struggling with. Alternatively you may feel you just need to strengthen these areas.

There can be many reasons that people feel that they are unable to cope with their life. For instance, some may feel they aren't strong enough to stand up to difficult or demanding people at work or at home, and situations might pile on the stress when you are least able to handle it. If you feel inadequate for any reason, a positive affirmation can help you become stronger.

Alternatively, you might want to work on your own emotions, especially negative ones, such as anger or jealousy. If you feel that your emotions are out of kilter, the meditations, grounding techniques, and affirmations in this chapter can help. Even if you feel reasonably happy about yourself but still want to bring some part of your mind or body into balance, the following meditations, grounding methods, and affirmations may be useful.

Included in each section are affirmations. These are positive words or statements that build and confirm good things about yourself. Examples would be, "I am strong" or "Who I am is good." They are meditations that need to be repeated in order to help guide and strengthen you into thinking positively about yourself. It is important to say each affirmation at least three times to allow it to sink in and take effect. For an even greater effect, repeat it three times, and then do another two sets of three.

It's best to repeat your affirmations in sets of three over a period of at least a few days, and preferably a few weeks, to feel their full benefit. With affirmations, if you are using a phrase or sentence, you must say that it is *already happening* ("I am strong"), not it *will happen* ("I will be strong"), as that suggests some time in the future, and your affirmations are intended to reinforce your positive feelings about yourself in the here and now.

Security

We all have an innate desire to live and survive on this planet. We have a natural instinct to provide ourselves with food, warmth, and shelter. We also have an built-in sense of danger and a basic sense of what we believe to be right or wrong.

When Balanced

- When balanced you feel confident about generating enough money, handling it properly, and you feel that you're in the right job, and you feel safe in your home.
- You feel happy about life.
- You are equally as happy in your own company as in the company of others.

When Out of Balance

- When insecure you can feel lonely.
- You can have an unfocused mind or feel spacey or out of touch with things.
- You can be either greedy about money or possessions or stingy about them.
- You have difficulty in caring for yourself and want others to look after you.
- You find it hard to cope with everyday life and achieving the basic things you need.

Affirmations

I am strong and independent.
I manage life easily.
I always have what I need.
Life becomes better and easier each day.

Wherever you are, stop and listen to the sound of your breathing. Now listen to the sounds around you. Keep listening until you have heard and counted five different sounds.

Grounding

Follow Key Meditation One: "Grounding" and add the following steps:

1. Send a thick taproot from the base of your spine.

2. Anchor this root into rock.

3. Bring your focus back up.

4. Center your focus just below your breastbone.

5. Lift or open your eyes.

Renewal

This meditation can help you to feel part of the world and the human race again, and it can activate your ability to get the basics of life together. Rather than visualizing anything in detail, it is better for you to focus on feeling that you are alive, here, and happy. For this meditation, you need ten to fifteen minutes of quiet privacy.

Connect Yourself Back to Life

1. Find a quiet place, sit and relax, close or lower your eyes.

2. Take your focus to your third eye.

3. Visualize the color indigo.

4. Now see the color clearing.

5. Visualize you are on a precipice looking at the earth from a distance.

6. You watch the planet as it begins to move closer to you.

7. As it approaches, it grows larger and larger.

8. Soon it is very close.

9. A white bridge forms, connecting the precipice to the earth.

10. You set off across the bridge.

11. It takes you through gentle clouds.

12. In front of you is a white wall with climbing plants growing up it.

13. There is an opening in the wall and the bridge takes you through it.

14. There is a gentle mist around you that fades and clears.

15. Around you are natural branches wound together.

16. You are in a tree house not far from the ground.

17. The branches form the sides and roof.

18. The floor is made up of soft, warm moss.

19. There is an open doorway and a short ladder to the ground.

20. Stay here until you feel ready to climb down the ladder.

21. When you do climb down, put bare feet on the ground.

22. Feel the creative earth energy drawing up into your feet.

23. Take a walk through a countryside of your choice.

24. Then return to your tree home.

25. When you are ready open your eyes.

Trusting

When you mistrust others, you harbor underlying feelings of not trusting yourself. We all come into this life trusting ourselves and knowing who is good for us and who is not, but we have also learned how to see ourselves and how to react to situations as a result of programming by our parents or family, and sometimes this is not how we would naturally be. We need to relearn how to trust our own instincts.

When Balanced

- You have self-control.
- You feel able to handle tricky situations positively and successfully.
- You are able to stand up for yourself when you feel you are right.
- You believe in what you do and what you say.

When Out of Balance

- You distrust the world or feel everyone rejects you.
- You don't trust your feelings, and therefore, you don't feel in control of your life.
- You don't trust yourself to do the right thing in situations.

- If you doubt or dislike yourself, you may act the victim or even display a cruel streak.
- You allow others to dominate you, as you don't have a will of your own.

Affirmations

Who I am is good.
I am in charge of my life.
I will always take care of me.
My decisions are good.

Admit Your Feelings

You can use the following meditation for looking into one feeling or for checking out a collection of emotions. It will help you uncover what you really think or feel, as opposed to what you have been taught to think and feel.

1. Sit quietly and close your eyes.

2. Allow a situation to run through your mind.

3. Focus on what you feel.

4. Admit to yourself what you feel.

5. Give yourself permission to have these feelings.

6. Now drain the feelings down your body.

7. Take them out through your feet.

8. Review a situation that concerns you.

9. Ask yourself what you want to happen.

10. When you feel you have an answer open your eyes.

When you want to blame someone else or feel you cannot cope with a situation, try this short meditation.

1. Relax and take a few deep breaths.

2. You see a stranger in your situation.

3. They tell you what is wrong.

4. Advise them, and tell them what they need to do in order to fix what is wrong.

5. Do they need input from another source? For instance, another person, a professional body, and so on.

6. What are the alternative methods?

7. Visualize them feeling strong and on top of the world while they sort themselves out.

8. Now apply this to you.

Stored Emotions

We all store our earliest feelings deep within us, and they influence the way we handle relationships and show our feelings. Whether we tend to feel rejected or accepted by others will shape our relationships and sexuality. Our emotions are important because our creative ideas spring from them; they show us what we want and allow us to feel that we belong in the world.

When Balanced

- Your emotions are genuine, honest, expressive, and giving.
- Your emotions are neither "over the top" nor too gushing.
- You express emotional and sexual needs naturally and don't overpower others with them.

When Out of Balance

- You are confused about what you feel and you don't trust your feelings.
- You suffer unnecessary guilt or self-disapproval.
- You feel sorry for yourself or play the martyr.
- You hold upset or anger inside for long periods and then just explode.
- You criticize yourself a lot.
- If you have lost someone close, your emotions can be oversensitive.

Affirmations

I listen to my feelings.
I trust what I feel.
I love and accept love easily.
I am happy sharing with my partner.
I love my sexuality.
I know my feelings.
I know myself.

Admit What You Feel

1. Find a quiet place and sit.

2. Follow the grounding exercise in Key Meditation One.

3. Focus on what is upsetting you.

4. Look at your feelings right now without deciding if they are right or wrong.

5. Just admit that you feel them and it is all right to feel them.

Healing Your Emotions

7

This meditation is useful if you have suffered from the breakup of a relationship. Use it if a partner has left you, if your partner has been deceitful, or if you have suffered any sort of rejection from someone you love, including friends or family.

The Artist's Studio

1. Find yourself a quiet space and sit with your eyes closed.

2. Imagine a white spinning light in the center of your forehead.

3. Enlarge the light and step through it.

4. Now see yourself in a clean white artist's studio.

5. Set a large white canvas in front of you.

6. Visualize a hurtful situation that is bothering you.

7. Freeze-frame it at the worst point as you saw it.

8. Paint in the person who has hurt you.

9. Paint in the surroundings you were in.

10. Paint in any other people involved, *excluding* yourself.

11. Drain the color out of the painting.

12. Turning all the images to black and white.

13. Shrink it down to a small square in the center of the canvas.

14. Take a paintbrush loaded with white paint.

15. Paint out the picture completely.

16. Open your eyes.

If you have had a series of upsetting events, paint the first event and shrink it, as instructed in the meditation, and then place it at the top left hand side of the canvas. Paint and shrink the next event, and line it up next to the first one. Continue in this manner, lining each one so that your canvas looks similar to an old black and white comic book. When you have finished, paint all the images out with a white paint brush.

Creating Confidence

Confidence gives us the faith to believe that we can achieve whatever we set out to do. We should be able to rely on ourselves, believe in ourselves, and believe in what we can do and achieve. This in turn will feed our self-esteem, self-respect and self-control. Confidence tends to waver up and down for everyone at times, so you need to know that you can bounce back after a setback.

When Balanced

- When you are confident you have faith in yourself.
- You are loyal to others and not afraid to try new things.
- Your energy is channeled in to what you want, whenever you want.
- You are not afraid to listen and trust your instincts.

When Out of Balance

- With a lack of confidence you feel inadequate to those around you.
- You can have addictive tendencies.
- You feel yourself to be the victim in life.
- Everyone else does better than you or has more than you.
- You can harbor feelings of jealousy or hostility toward others.
- You may feel suspicious or even paranoid of other people.
- There are feelings of intimidation by the achievements of others.

Affirmations

I believe in me.
I need only my own approval.
My achievements get better and better.
I deal with everything well.
I deal with life well.
I love new experiences.

Golden Moments

1. Find a quiet place, sit, and close your eyes.

2. Take a couple of deep breaths and relax.

3. Think of the things you have accomplished from childhood to adulthood.

4. You rode a bike, learned to swim, passed exams, learned to drive.

5. Visualize yourself imprinting a picture of the golden moment on the pages of a large book.

6. Think of one or two more of these achievements.

7. Record them in the book.

8. When you have finished, close the book.

9. Put it in a safe place for future use.

10. When you're ready, open your eyes.

After this meditation it is a good idea to actually begin a real scrapbook of your achievements. You can then visualize the pages when you repeat this meditation.

Give Yourself a Boost

1. Find a quiet time for a few moments.

2. Relax and take a few deep in breaths.

3. Think of a person to whom you feel inferior, and visualize them as larger than you.

4. See them standing next to you, painted in a vibrant color.

5. You grow, rising up to the same size.

6. You too are now made up of the same vibrant colors.

7. The other person now disappears.

Self Esteem

We are all born with a natural tendency to like and accept ourselves, which means that as children, we are open with our feelings and actions. Ideally we should continue with this as adults. However, constant criticism can give us feelings of inadequacy, especially if they are endured over a long period. Even when nothing is said, feeling silent disdain from others can be just as damaging to our self-esteem.

When Balanced

- When you like yourself you treat yourself with care and respect.
- You do not blame yourself for every mishap that happens in your life, you accept that bad things can happen.
- You see yourself as a competent, together person and realize your limitations.

When Out of Balance

- You listen to the "put-downs" of others and take them to heart.
- You feel you have let someone down by not meeting his or her high expectations of you.
- You let others control you or you try to control others.
- You feel inadequate next to a sibling or close friend who is a higher achiever or a favorite.
- You feel worthless.
- You cannot forgive your past mistakes.

Affirmations

I value everything about me.
I deserve respect and happiness.
I am unique.
I am free to be me.
I am worth it.

Meditation for a Potentially Difficult Day

1. As you begin your day, sit on the edge of the bed.

2. Stretch your arms and take a couple of deep breaths.

3. Visualize a round golden shield, covering your navel and abdomen.

4. The surface of the shield is reflective and nothing can penetrate.

5. Visualize it staying in place all day.

If you are laboring under excessive criticism, try the following exercise while the person is criticizing you.

1. Turn your head so that they are speaking into only one ear.

2. Lower your eyes and picture their words going in one ear, through your head, and out of the other ear.

3. Take your focus away from the words and just watch the flow of energy moving through and out the other side.

4. Drain all of the energy out of your head when they have gone.

Rebuilding Your Self Worth

1. Find a quiet place you will not be disturbed.

2. Relax, close your eyes, and take a few deep breaths.

3. Take your focus to your third eye.

4. Visualize a circle filled with purple mist.

5. Step through the center.

6. You are on a path on a bright sunny day.

7. The path meanders through a lovely garden.

8. The path leads you to a pool.

9. Sit and look at your reflection.

10. Tell yourself the good qualities about yourself.

11. Tell yourself all the things you have achieved recently.

12. Congratulate yourself.

13. Leave the pool and take the path back through the garden.

14. Step back through the purple mist.

15. When you are ready, open your eyes.

Love Others and Love Yourself

How we give, show, and accept love from others affects all of our relationships, as does (just as importantly) the love and care we give to ourselves. Love boosts our morale, our ability to cope with dilemmas, and also our ability to hope.

When Balanced

- You are honest in love, honest with your feelings.
- You feel others are genuine and honest with you.
- You can laugh and cry naturally, not holding back your feelings.
- You are happy giving love and don't expect great things in return.
- You accept and love others for who they are, not what you would like them to be.

When Out of Balance

- You cannot move on from hurts.
- You feel unworthy to be loved by anybody.
- You harbor fears of loneliness or betrayal or both.
- You automatically push your own needs to the background.
- You are stingy with others or you deny yourself simple treats and joys in life.
- You are being dishonest in a relationship and dishonest with yourself.
- There is a constant need to change others rather than to accept them for who they are.

Affirmations

I love who I am.

I am attractive to others.

It is easy to love me.

Love is all around me.

Love is always flowing through my life.

When you are sorting out matters of love, if you can find the real reason or the underlying truth of what has happened, you are free to improve the situation or move on.

Focusing on Yourself

1. Find a quiet moment and relax.

2. Take a few deep breaths, close your eyes.

3. Focus on a relationship in which you are feeling unbalanced.

4. Look at your part in the relationship.

5. Ask yourself what your feelings are.

6. Delve down to your real feelings and reasons for your unhappiness and irritation.

7. Be honest with yourself.

Focusing on the Other Person

1. Take a few deep breaths.

2. Focus on a relationship in which you are feeling unbalanced.

3. Look at the other person.

4. Determine whether the other person has expressed his or her true feelings.

5. Does this person's words match his or her actions?

Deep Meditation—What Makes you Happy?

This meditation can be very effective if you record it over a favorite piece of music. It will have a strong effect if you practice it morning and night for a week or two.

1. Relax, take a few deep in breaths, and close your eyes.

2. Take your focus down to the middle of your chest.

3. Open a golden door and follow a golden corridor to a place that you love.

4. Waiting for you is someone with whom you have a special bond.

5. You talk with them about what really makes you happy.

6. You discuss desires you have that are heartfelt, and the thoughts that make you happy.

7. Discuss the things that interest and fulfill you.

8. You both agree to meet again.

9. You return along the corridor and through the door.

10. Close the door and open your eyes.

Communication

We communicate with others in many ways—by what we say, what we do, by our facial expressions, and through our body language. By the way we talk, we show what we feel, what we agree with, or whether we accept or like whomever we are talking to. The world communicates back to us, not only through speech but also through our other sensory organs, such as the eyes, ears, and nose. We need to communicate clearly with others and we need to know how to express ourselves. Poor communication can lead to people misunderstanding us, and being afraid to communicate can leave us isolated and lonely.

When Balanced

- You speak and think clearly and communicate in a non-threatening way.
- You will see your mistakes and be able to formulate solutions.
- You can be happy to listen to others as well as be the one who talks.
- Your sincerity is apparent and you say what you mean.
- Your senses are alert and sharp.

When Out of Balance

- A common block is only seeing only what you want to see or hearing what you want to hear.
- When you gossip.
- By saying one thing and doing another.
- You scheme and manipulate others through talk.
- You have a tendency to burst out with wild statements.
- If you are too picky or fault finding.
- You hold back from speaking up for yourself.
- You fail to express your emotions or opinions when asked.

Affirmations

I love expressing myself.
I always speak what I feel.
I speak my truth.
It is safe for me to speak my feelings.
What I say is worth hearing.
My voice is heard.

A Humming Meditation

Humming and singing are good for clearing the voice. Talking and singing loudly help you develop confidence in your ability to speak up. So if you have swallowed what you have wanted to say recently, try this meditation.

1. When you have some time to yourself, hum one tone emphasizing the *mmm* sound in your throat.

2. Change the tone, but again emphasize the *mmm* sound.

3. Practice *oms*, elongating the *mm* and feeling it in your throat.

4. Play a song or piece of music and hum each note.

5. Now focus on building volume as you are humming.

6. Now sing a song you know well—loudly!

If you are frightened of saying what you want or what you feel in a situation, try this meditation.

1. Relax, take a few deep breaths, and lengthen the out breath.

2. Lower or close your eyes.

3. Visualize yourself in the situation where you are facing the other person.

4. See yourself saying ridiculous things that may be truths or utter nonsense.

5. Say things that you would never say.

6. Continue until you find it too humorous to continue.

7. Now visualize their reaction.

8. Now visualize them doing this with you.

9. Now see if what you are holding back is still so daunting.

10. When you are ready open your eyes.

Self-Motivation

There are times when our sources of inspiration dry up, and there are also occasions when even the most wonderful career loses its allure and we find ourselves bored or frustrated. The solution is to look around for a new job or a fresh project, but sometimes that is not possible, so you need something to help you keep going. We all need to create aims and goals that give us purpose and inspiration in life, and when we lose our urge to go forward in life, we have lost our ability to create new goals. This leads us to becoming stuck in a situation. The following affirmations will help you tap into some initiative and find some balance until you can find a new direction.

When Balanced

- You are happy, inspired and motivated
- There is a healthy interest in your path through life and a drive to progress.
- You are moving forward in life.
- Your goals are realistic and you stick to them.

When Out of Balance

- You go around in circles in life.
- You find it hard to move forward with anything.
- There is a tendency to start things but never finish them.
- You feel disillusioned.
- You find it hard to raise enthusiasm and lose interest in things easily

Affirmations

There is much of life to explore.

I am free to move forward.

Today I will change my life.

I am open to new directions.

Happiness lies in new ideas.

To Help You Find a New Direction

Choose a favorite piece of music that you have found to be inspiring and play it.

1. As the music begins, relax with a few deep in breaths.

2. Close your eyes.

3. Clear your mind and just listen to the music.

4. Feel the melody taking you forward.

5. Visualize two golden doors opening.

6. You go through onto a brighter path forward.

7. When the music finishes, slowly open your eyes and align with *now*.

Then . . .

1. Sit quietly, relax, and close your eyes.

2. Look at the main areas of your life.

3. Look at your work. Is it what you want?

4. Then your home. Are you where you want to be?

5. Next your relationships. Are you happy in them?

6. Can you create ways for these areas of your life to move forward?

7. Visualize where you would like to be in one year's time.

8. Visualize where you want to be in five years' time.

9. When you have formulated your aims, open your eyes.

Begin a notebook of plans for your work, home, and relationships, and note down ways in which all these areas of your life can move forward.

The Real You

It is calming, strengthening, and inspiring when we let ourselves be who we really are. Some people believe that life is a journey that is designed to allow us to discover our true selves. Whatever you believe, when you are happy and feel good about yourself, it follows that you can create a fulfilled and happy life.

When Balanced

- Your clothes, appearance, and home will suit who you are.
- You allow yourself to be creative in the way you dress.
- You will know and accept what makes you happy and strive to incorporate this into your lifestyle.
- You know how to pace yourself with work and projects and you know your limitations.

When Out of Balance

- When out of touch with yourself you will feel lost.
- You will set your sights too low when aiming for goals.
- You find yourself living by someone else's set of rules.
- You give yourself little attention.

Affirmations

I enjoy discovering me.
I will look and dress like who I am.
I am going forward.
I love my creative side.
I am creative with myself.
I strive to make myself happy.

To Attract a Better Future

Imagine all the restrictions have gone from your life: for instance, shortage of money, responsibilities, and commitments to anything or anyone. With this in view, follow this meditation and as far as you can, visualize it in detail.

1. Relax, take a few deep breaths, and close your eyes.

2. Take your focus to your third eye.

3. Visualize a spinning circular disk, growing larger.

4. Walk through the center.

5. You are redecorating your bedroom.

6. You are getting new furniture.

7. How will it look?

8. Your wardrobe is empty.

9. With what clothes will you fill it?

10. You blend with the spinning white light of your third eye.

11. When you are ready, open your eyes.

And now . . .

1. Relax, take a few deep breaths, and close your eyes.

2. Take your focus to your third eye.

3. Visualize a spinning circular disc, growing larger.

4. Walk through the center.

5. You are given the chance of embarking on an interesting journey.

6. To which country would it be?

7. What would you like to see and experience?

8. Visualize that you are making that journey.

9. When you have finished, return.

10. Blend with the spinning white light of your third eye.

11. When you are ready, open your eyes.

And again . . .

1. Relax, take a few deep breaths, and close your eyes.

2. Take your focus to your third eye.

3. Visualize a spinning circular disc, growing larger.

4. Walk through the center.

5. You are invited to a social occasion.

6. There you meet someone you have admired from afar.

7. You have the chance to talk to this person.

8. What would you want to talk to them about?

9. Why does this person interest or inspire you?

10. You are asked what you feel is your goal or mission in life.

11. What would you reply?

12. You blend with the spinning white light of your third eye.

13. When you are ready, open your eyes.

Let Yourself Live

Life is to be lived, experienced, enjoyed. Fun, happiness, and new experiences should be consistent throughout your life, and it is up to you to make sure they are! We are all constantly growing, both mentally and emotionally, and as we grow so our lives move forward. If we stunt our growth, then in turn our lives will become stunted.

When Balanced

- You see life as an adventure with new opportunities.
- You take charge and work toward making yourself happy.
- You decide whom to allow in your life, how much you are involved with them, and how much of your time they will share.
- You decide what or who will affect you and your actions.

When Out of Balance

- It is all work and no play.
- You resort to analyzing situations too much.
- You find it hard to let go and enjoy yourself.
- There is a constant "wanting" or waiting for something.

- Your life is at a standstill.
- You could harbor a strong fear of dying or a fear of living.
- You limit yourself or see life as limited.

Affirmations

I am unique and happy.
I am growing and transforming my life.
I am creating a new future.
I am allowing fun into everyday.
This is the first day of the rest of my life.
Today I will change my life.

Change One Thing

1. Relax, take a few long breaths, and close your eyes.

2. Visualize yourself holding a clear crystal sphere in which you can see an aspect of your life (work, friends, home, money, chores, children).

3. In the aspect of your life that you have chosen to focus on, ask yourself how could you take one step forward.

4. When you feel you have an answer, open your eyes.

5. Write it down.

Color
Healing

8

There are many energies buzzing around our planet that we come in contact with everyday, such as electrical, nuclear, gravitational, and weather-related. Every living being gives out energy, along with some things that we may not expect to do this, such as rocks, crystals, and colors. In addition, our thoughts and our feelings create energy. Happy thoughts and feelings are good for our health, while negative ones create energies that make us feel bad. By balancing our thought and feelings, the energy in our bodies can change and heal us.

In the 1970s, scientists studied some of the trained meditation experts of the East and discovered that the mind has a powerful effect on the body. They also discovered that our nervous system affects the body's immune system. Emotional and psychological stress can weaken the body's defense against illness, but by calming the mind and lightening stress, meditation can help to bolster our immune systems.

Color is composed of light of varying wavelengths or frequencies that create an energy or vibration. Different colors vibrate at different frequencies, releasing different types of energy. For example, the energy of blue is calming and cooling and the energy of red is warming and invigorating. Meditating on certain colors can link us into their energy and this can help us to heal and balance certain aspects of our bodies and our lives.

A simple way of meditating with color is to collect colored cards or papers (pure hues, that are sold in art and craft shops are best). Pick a color that you are drawn to and just sit quietly and look at the color for several minutes until you feel ready to stop. You can use colored bulbs to light the area in which you meditate to enhance the meditation. If you find yourself feeling low or over-emotional, check to see if you have been wearing a lot of dark colors over recent weeks. The color of your bedding and color around you in your home can also have an effect on you.

The Chakras

One cannot talk about color healing without discussing the chakras—the seven vortices of life energy in our bodies—since each of these is associated with a color. Keeping our chakras cleared and in balance affects our physical health, and opening the chakras are the gateway to spiritual and psychic advancement. Chapter 12, which focuses on advanced meditation techniques, will present methods of chakra opening in more detail. In this chapter, we will focus on the importance of the color itself.

Much of the focus of healing through meditation is concerned with developing the "heart energy," so whether you feel this energy as peace, joy, love, or devotion, it is the same basic energy. Developing our "heart energy" can prevent us from feeling separate or alien from other people. It is a strong mind and body healer. The most effective way to bring happiness and love into your life is to use your heart center energy to generate love for yourself, as this has the effect of drawing love and happiness from the world into your heart.

It has been found that visualizing color during meditation can be very healing, as each color will resonate its associated chakra and help you regain energy balance, which in turn has a strong healing effect.

Crown Chakra: Purple

Brow Chakra: Indigo blue

Throat Chakra: Turquoise

Heart Chakra: Green

Solar Plexus Chakra: Yellow

Sacral Chakra: Orange

Base Chakra: Red

There are three colors that are regarded as powerful healers, and these are known as "universal healing colors." These are green, orange, and blue. Each creates a healing effect or vibration and each works in a different way.

Green Meditation: Heart Chakra

Green is the color connected to your heart chakra and it comes through your heart center.

At birth, you come into life with an open heart and you love and accept people and things easily. Then, like most humans, you later learn to close your heart a bit in order to protect yourself from hurt, upset, or feelings of threat. Meditation with your heart energy takes you back to your real self, to knowing who you were before the layers of hurt and fear built up. The heart chakra meditation is beneficial because it takes your emotional calendar back in time.

Green is nature's healing and growth color. As nature is balanced, so too can the color green help balance your life, promoting clear perspective. Physically, green offers healing to nervous disorders, an overactive thyroid, and high blood pressure. Blood circulates through the heart, so green is helpful for arteries, veins, and major organs in the body such as the liver.

1. Sit in a quiet place and relax with a few deep breaths.

2. Making your breaths out longer than your inward breaths.

3. Close your eyes and focus on a white beam of light shining down.

4. You are in the center of a white spotlight.

5. The white light turns emerald green, entering your body through the back of your heart center.

6. Your heart fills with emerald green light.

7. Send out a shard of green energy from your heart center to a part of your body you feel needs healing.

8. Allow the green to wrap around the organ or area.

9. Visualize that part of your body turning green.

10. Leave the energy there.

11. Repeat this to a second organ or area.

12. When you have finished, leave the energy in your heart.

13. Close the back of your heart by closing an imaginary camera shutter.

14. Send the spotlight of light up into the sky.

15. When you are ready, open your eyes.

Pink can also be used with this meditation by following it with pink after doing it with green. Pale to mid-pink soothes emotional hurts. It is good for releasing feelings of neglect or anger triggered by emotional betrayal or disappointments. To inspire a stronger sense of love for others use a deep pink in the heart center.

Please note: green is not suitable for healing tumors or cancer as it encourages growth. Red is good for these as it burns out cancer cells, heals diseases of the blood, heals wounds and also helps with depression.

Orange Meditation: Sacral Chakra

Orange is the color of emotional healing, and it can be effective on deep levels. Focusing on the color orange in meditation can ease emotional trauma or an old hurt that you find difficult to let go of. Orange can also help with bereavement. Orange is also a good color for building up the immune system and building up your body after an illness. It increases motivation and sexual energy. Orange can also help with pneumonia, multiple sclerosis, the reproductive system, and the kidneys.

1. Find yourself a relaxing, quiet place to sit.

2. Close your eyes and take in some long, deep breaths.

3. Focus on making the out breaths longer as this will help to calm fraught feelings.

4. Take your focus down to the base of your spine and visualize a white spiral of light growing down from the base of your backbone.

5. The spiral grows downward into the earth, going deeper and deeper.

6. You have reached the orange glow of the earth's center.

7. At this point, see the light changing from white to orange.

8. Pull the orange energy up your spiral cord and into the base of your back.

9. The orange energy flows into the lower part of your backbone and rises up to just below waist level.

10. From the backbone, the orange glow radiates forward filling your abdomen, until this area of your body is full of the orange energy.

11. Feel this warm, gentle energy soothe you for several minutes.

12. The energy clears from your abdomen back into your backbone.

13. Then it drains back down the spiral cord, returning the energy to the earth's center.

14. Pull up the spiral of light up through the earth and back into your backbone.

15. When you are ready, open your eyes.

Note: Too much use of orange can antagonize mental distress. Use orange sparingly if there are mental issues involved such as low self-esteem or a temporary loss of confidence.

Blue Meditation: Throat Chakra

Babies come into the world in touch with their spiritual selves, which is partly why they carry light blue in their aura or energy field. Blue has a higher vibration of healing, purifying at the spiritual level. Blue calms the thoughts, soothes emotions, and eases physical troubles. It reduces agitation and has a cooling effect that acts as a sedative for the body. In spiritual terms, blue is an "antiseptic" color that helps strengthen the immune system.

Blue is physically useful for underactive thyroids, fevers, and burns, nausea, and sore throats!

1. Find a quiet, peaceful place and close your eyes.

2. Take some deep in breaths and longer out breaths until you feel relaxed.

3. Take your focus to your third eye.

4. Visualize a white spinning disc that grows larger and larger.

5. It grows large enough for you to step through.

6. As you watch, the white disc turns a vibrant royal blue.

7. As you walk toward the disc, you see it is made up of blue mist.

8. Walk into the mist and feel it enter the front of you and sweep right through you, turning you royal blue.

9. Your skin, hair, muscles, and bones turn blue.

10. As you step out of the mist, feel it leave the back of you.

11. Turn and walk through the mist a second time, experiencing the color sweep through you again.

12. Let it blend with your body.

13. When you are ready, open your eyes.

Color as a Purifier

Meditating on certain colors sweeping through your body can be like washing your system through on the inside, then energizing it. The following colors are good for just that. Imagine these colors as mists that you walk through (as in the blue meditation), or as a color that enters the top of your head, and which you then draw down your body on the inside from the top of your head to your feet. You can visualize parts of your body, such as the skeleton, organs, muscles, or skin, turning various colors as a method of healing.

White Meditation

White is made up of all the colors of the spectrum, and it is highly cleansing. It clears away stored negative energy in the mind, body, and spirit. It can amplify and strengthen healing if used at the beginning and end of a color healing meditation. It purifies, eases conditions, including physical pain, and gives spiritual calmness and comfort. Physically white can help heal headaches and skin ailments, also depression, exhaustion, and it can help those who have epilepsy.

For healing with white light, please see the Key Meditation Two: "White Light," on page 22.

Using white light to heal another person can be very effective, and other colors can be used to supplement it. When doing this, ask your friend to sit on a chair. You stand behind the chair. Place your hands on your client's shoulders and visualize white light coming down into the top of your head, down through your head along your shoulders, down your arms, and out of your palms. Allow the light to flow into the person, moving your hands if you feel you want to. If you then would like to use another color let it come through your head and onto your client. Follow your intuition to decide what colors to use and when to stop.

Silver Meditation

Silver works as a purifier in the same way as white, but it can break down areas of debris in the energy field (the aura). Silver can speed up your vibration, helping you achieve better concentration during meditating. This color triggers inspiration for creative projects such as art, music, and writing, so it can be useful to meditate on silver if you have a creative block.

It is beneficial to perform the white meditation before the silver meditation. Follow these steps for the silver mediation.

1. Sit in a quiet place, relax, and close your eyes.

2. Take your focus to your third eye.

3. Visualize your reflection in a round mirror.

4. Around your body you can see a ring of energy.

5. Take note of any gray or dark areas.

6. Fill the ring of energy with silver.

7. Watch the discolored areas melt away as the silver filters through them.

8. Now see the silver color begin to penetrate your skin.

9. Visualize yourself stepping into the mirror and blending with your image.

10. When you feel happy you have blended with your reflection step back out of the mirror.

11. Take one final look in the mirror and see your energy field turn to gold.

12. The mirror returns to a white spinning disc.

13. Take your focus down to just below the center of your rib cage.

14. When you are ready open your eyes.

Gold Meditation

Gold has been highly regarded since ancient times when people believed it to be sunshine that had become solid metal. It has a very fine frequency of energy that puts us in touch with what is going on around us. It is the best color to repel or disperse negative energy. It is the most uplifting color for lightening heavy moods and it should be used gradually at first because of its strong vibration.

1. Sit quietly, relax, and close your eyes.

2. Take one or two deep breaths.

3. Send up a thought for a golden shaft of light to come from a high point in the sky.

4. As it reaches you, it turns into hundreds of raindrops that shower through you and your energy field.

5. Negative energy washes away into the ground.

6. When you have finished, send the light back.

7. Open your eyes.

Turquoise Meditation

Turquoise can provide emotional or physical healing, but I suggest you use it as a form of psychic protection. After using the gold, silver, and white meditations, it is good to finish with turquoise. Visualize yourself putting on a vibrant turquoise cloak with a large hood that falls over and covers your third eye. Fasten up the front so that your body is covered. You can put on two, three, or more cloaks, one on top of another until you feel thoroughly protected. Alternatively, you could imagine yourself getting into a turquoise sleeping bag and zipping it up all around you.

Nature
Meditations

9

The countryside and unspoiled landscapes have a calm, untouched, non-chaotic energy that allows you to still your thoughts and emotions. The color green is abundant in nature, and as this is the color of your heart center, it can restore you back to your natural self or give you self-awareness. Nature is straightforward and uncomplicated, yet always busy creating and growing. People relax outdoors, but also see nature a source of inspiration, with activities such as rock climbing, hiking, and sailing. These days, it is often good just to breathe some fresh air.

Beautiful natural scenes of landscapes or waterscapes have a calming and healing effect, and birds and animals can help heal and empower you. When using nature for meditation, make the meditation more effective by focusing on an ideal natural place. If you can actually go to a favorite spot and focus on the scene, try to absorb as much in detail as you can, so you have a strong memory that you can tap into later for meditation purposes.

Earth

The earth contains a very creative energy. Plants grow from the earth, and water springs from beneath rocks. The earth absorbs negative energy, which it is able to change from negative to positive. We see this in the cycle of nature as things grow, mature, grow old and die, and sink back into the ground, from which new life springs from the nutrients.

Earth Meditation One

1. Visualize your feet are buried in the earth up to your ankles.

2. Earth energy is being pulled up through the arches in your feet, then through your legs into your tummy.

3. Allow it to drain back out.

Earth Meditation Two

1. You are on a camel riding across the golden sands of a desert.

2. The sun is warm, and you approach a settlement.

3. Brightly colored tents stretch out in front of you.

4. The desert sand ends and you jump down feeling warm soft earth under your bare feet.

5. You lead your camel to drink fresh water.

6. There are large bathing pools of shallow mud where you lay and cover your whole body in warm soft purifying mud.

7. You can feel negative energy drawing out through your skin and being absorbed by the mud.

8. You wash the mud off under a gentle waterfall.

9. Mount the camel and set off again in the sunshine.

Water

Water is an emotional healer, and visualizing any type of natural water source, for instance, waterfalls, lakes, or the sea, is beneficial.

This meditation works on a deep, emotional, healing level, helping you clear away old hurts, distresses, and anxieties. It is useful when you find it difficult to move on from an emotionally harrowing situation. Practicing this meditation can help you heal and strengthen.

1. Sit quietly and focus on deep breathing.

2. Close your eyes and take your focus to your third eye.

3. Open a white camera shutter and move through it.

4. Visualize yourself standing at the foot of a gentle waterfall and hear the sound of water running down the rocks.

5. A pool is gathering at the foot of the waterfall.

6. You step toward the pool and put your bare feet in the water.

7. Visualize two camera shutters opening in the soles of your feet and draw the water right up your body to the top of your head.

8. When you are completely full of water, let the water drain back out through your feet.

9. Close the camera shutters in the soles of your feet.

10. Step out of the pool.

11. Feel yourself blend back into your body.

12. When you are ready open your eyes.

Mountains

Mountains are still, strong, solid, and immobile. This meditation is ideal if you feel you are being carried along by fast moving events. Perhaps you feel uncertain of yourself or feel that you need to step back from a situation and reassess it. This meditation is helpful if you feel you have spent too long trying to achieve something and you are losing faith.

1. Find a quiet place to either sit or stand.

2. Focus on your favorite hill or mountain or imagine your own beautiful large soaring mountain.

3. You are outside on a bright sunny day standing on a path leading you to your mountain.

4. Picture yourself growing as large as the mountain.

5. Absorb yourself into the mountain and feel the strong still base, the large circular width, and the strength with which it supports its own weight.

6. Imagine the timeless stillness of a mountain being formed many thousands of years ago and remaining for thousands of years to come.

7. Allow the strength and stillness to absorb into your being.

8. You are calm and strong.

9. As you feel yourself become the mountain, allow your eyes to look out from the pinnacle and your vision takes in views from all around.

10. You see clearly all that is taking place for miles.

11. You have the time to observe and see all that is occurring.

12. You will remain strong and steady with your progress.

13. Feel your self come out of the mountain and return to normal size.

14. Walk back along the path and in through the spinning light into your third eye.

15. When you feel centered in your body, open your eyes.

Trees

Trees are seen as a form of energy or life. You will make this meditation more effective by actually doing it in a forest. If this isn't practical, go to a park where there are trees or to a wooded area, and absorb the scene into your mind's eye so that you can later visualize it when you have the peace and time to meditate on it. Vary the experience from time to time, so that you visit the wood at different times of year and at different times of day, as the energy of early morning will be very different from the energy of the evening, and springtime will feel different from winter. This is a long meditation, so you might want to record it and then follow the recording for your meditation.

1. Complete Key Meditation One: "Grounding," on page 20.

2. Take your focus to your third eye and visualize a white spinning disc.

3. You watch the disc growing larger and larger, and when it is big enough step through it.

4. Stretched out in front of you is a sunny country scene with trees, hedgerows, grassy fields, and a path.

5. You begin to walk along a path that meanders into very pretty woodland, with shafts of sunlight falling through the trees.

6. As you walk through the woodland you see old and new trees and wild flowers.

7. You come across a clearing and walk into the center where there is a large old tree with a thick trunk.

8. You sit, leaning back on the tree and relax.

9. As you look around be aware of the time of day and the season.

10. Focus on the sounds you hear in the forest.

11. What do you smell?

12. What do you taste?

13. What do you see around you?

14. Is the air warm and still or is a gentle breeze blowing across your face?

15. Put your hands on the ground.

16. What are you touching?

17. Your feet are bare what do you feel under them?

18. Put your hands on the bark of the tree and feel the texture.

19. Take your focus now to the tree and begin to blend in with it; feel yourself extend down into the deep roots, pulling up food, water, and the natural earth energy.

20. Now rise up the trunk, feeling yourself stretching into the branches.

21. Feel the solid strength of the tree, the stillness of the tree, and the sunlight absorbing into the leaves.

22. Look out at the forest from the top of the tree, as the tree would view the forest.

23. Feel yourself now coming down from the high branches and up from the roots, shrinking to your normal size inside the tree.

24. Now come out of the tree and imagine yourself once again sitting and leaning against the trunk.

25. Connect again with being on the ground of the forest, viewing the woodland from your normal vision level.

26. When you are ready, stand up and make your way out of the clearing, back onto the path, and out of the forest.

27. Now return back in through your third eye and back into yourself.

28. When you are ready, open your eyes.

Power Animals

Power animals are used in shamanism, which itself is the world's oldest healing practice. Shamanic elements can be found in all cultures, particularly in healing meditations or meditation and "journeys" made by the Native American tribes and the ancient Celtic peoples of Britain, Northern Europe, Russia, and Scandinavia, and within the indigenous tribes of Africa and Australia.

The shaman, or medicine worker, will work with power animals to heal. When meditating with power animals, you go on a visualized journey, either as the animal or with the animal, to experience a natural way of being, because animals and birds are not complicated in themselves and they do not complicate their lives. We may lose natural ways of surviving hardships, but by meditating on power animals we can pick up on their positive energy. Power animals are always wild creatures, and may be anything from insects, reptiles, sea creatures, to birds and mammals. They help give direction and purpose to life. They free you from the assumption that you are a helpless victim of circumstance or that fate controls your life. Meditation with power animals connects you with nature, to discover who you are and what your purpose is in this life.

When using power animals for healing meditation, you may wish to imagine the animal as it looks just after it is born, then using your mind's eye, watch it grow into a mature animal. For instance if you use a bird for your meditation, first imagine the egg, the egg hatching as a chick, the chick becoming a fledgling, and finally growing into an adult bird. This type of visualization can be difficult, especially if you do not have a lot of personal experience observing animals, but this "growth" meditation can strengthen your overall meditation experience.

The Bear

Bears are thought to know the planet as a living being, and Native American and other traditions say that they can connect us to the

heartbeat of mother earth. Their energy protects us from harm and from negative energy given out by others in the same way that a parent protects a child. Bears are also associated with knowledge and understanding of dreams and daydreams. By using either polar bears or brown bears in meditation we can set up protection for ourselves from the negative energy of others. Mothers give their children teddy bears, and although this tradition is only around 100 years old, the bear is an ancient symbol of protection during the night.

The Brown Bear

Brown bears hibernate and spend much of their time asleep, so a brown bear meditation can help dispel fears of the dark or being alone. This kind of meditation helps us to heal our inner child, which is the core or child in us that our adult traits are based on. These bears live in caves, which are believed to represent the womb of mother earth. Brown bears symbolize a link with rocks and minerals found in caves and to healing crystals.

The Polar Bear

In a meditation, a polar bear is considered to provide a healing and nurturing influence that protects you when your family has failed you. These loving yet protective bears can help you feel you are part of the world. Wonderfully fluid when they swim, they are connected to the element of water and thus to all types of emotional healing. They can survive in very barren cold landscapes, helping you to survive loneliness and separation.

The Wolf

In a meditation, a wolf is connected to the idea of protection when you venture into new places, either as part of a group or on your own. The wolf is swift, alert, and strong and it can be a pack animal or a loner. It has powerful instincts and a talent for survival.

The Deer

The healing aspect of the deer is the idea of mending difficult situations, by helping you to calm down and listen to others. Deer excel at watching and listening because they are alert and wary. They have sharp instincts, they can smell danger and they are associated with the concept of clairvoyance. Unless disturbed, they live in the present, in a gentle, peaceful, and graceful way that is in complete harmony with their surroundings.

The Frog

The frog image in a meditation offers healing and cleansing to the emotions and feelings, therefore it aids you when suffering from worry, stress, and nervousness. Frogs live in the "emotional" element of water, and are very flexible and adaptable, so this energy can be used to help you become less rigid with your emotions. Frogs start life as eggs, and then become tadpoles and eventually frogs. Meditate on being the tadpole, then see yourself grow into the frog, and as you do so this will symbolically help your character to develop and grow stronger.

Birds and Insects

Birds in shamanic healing are seen to be balancing as they fly, using two wings of equal size on either side of their bodies. They fly high and observe the things from an elevated viewpoint, which offers them a clear picture. They are also spiritually and intuitively strengthening.

The Eagle

The eagle is the high-flier among birds and it is considered the most spiritual, so it connects you to guides and helpers in the spirit worlds. The eagle can take you way above this world and strengthen your spirit. This large bird brings strength, courage, and wisdom and rises above the material world of money and possessions. She sees the bigger picture of what life is all about.

The Raven

Meditate on the raven when you need healing or after an upsetting or traumatic situation, as this bird-meditation can help remove
fear. The raven is able to find light in the
darkness; therefore it guides you when you
feel lost. The raven endows you with the

strength to change or tear down what needs to be rebuilt in your
life, thus it can help you get over a bad relationship, and help you
find a decent job after time spent in the wrong line of work. It can
help you overcome unhealthy or addictive habits.

The Owl

The owl can transform your thoughts and feelings from low or
bad to good and happy. The owl is silent and swift, and she can
see behind the masks that people put up to hide their real selves.
This bird meditation will help you to secrets or hidden agendas
that can harm you, but it will also help you to keep good secrets.
The owl can improve your powers of insight when your vision
in a situation is cloudy. You can meditate on an owl to solve a
problem, but it's best to focus on only one problem with each
owl meditation, even though owls can turn their heads in a full
circle seeing all around them, dealing with more than one thing
will complicate matters.

The Swan

Swans are believed to understand love and heart to heart con-
tacts, so swan meditations are helpful when you want to heal

hurts that arise from partners and relationships. Swans transform from ugly cygnets to graceful, large beautiful birds who mate for life. Swans live on water, and water is what psychics consider the "feeling or emotional" element, so this makes them sensitive to emotions. Swans will show you how you can attract your physical partner. Meditate on yourself as though you were an adult swan, meeting with your swan mate.

The Hummingbird

This little bird is symbolic of joy and happiness, so a meditation on this heals painful love situations. When you meditate on this bird, visualize a ray of healing light coming from its mouth.

The Butterfly

A butterfly meditation will heal shock and trauma, helping you to face things you have never faced before and to create a new beginning if you need to. Always moving, constantly active, their energy is transforming, changing weak thoughts and feelings into

strong ones. Butterflies bring change for the better. In ancient Greece the butterfly symbolized a free soul. Butterflies can represent great change and a positive outcome after you have been taken to the brink of disaster. Butterflies are seen as bringers of magic, because of their metamorphism from a slow crawling creature to a beautiful flying insect. They inspire solutions that come in unexpected ways.

Using Power Animals for Protection

You can use the energies of any power animal for protection by visualizing your chosen animal as a kind of cloak around you. The head becomes your head, the animal's front legs or wings become your arms, and the animal becomes your body. By doing this several times, or with several animal images, you will feel a protective layer of energy developing around you. In shamanic beliefs, individuals should take on the energies of animals that frighten us, such as spiders, snakes, and mice, because confronting these creatures in meditation will heal us on many psychological levels. You could visualize yourself doing the *nice* things that they do, such as spinning webs, shedding shimmering skins, or happily scampering around a field.

The
Healing
Room

10

This meditation enables you to create an inner "healing room" or place that you can return to in your mind whenever you want to. Although the meditation represents a complete healing cycle, you can build on or add your own very personal healing buy putting a picture, photo or special object on a table or shelf nearby while you meditate. The meditation is designed to strengthen your intuition by exercising your psychic senses, as well as clearing your system of suppressed negative energy. This will give you deep emotional healing and recharge your energy levels.

The time duration of this meditation is approximately thirty-five minutes and there is a sequence of healing methods. You will gain the maximum benefit by recording this meditation on tape.

You can do this meditation sitting or lying down. To receive the full benefit of this meditation, first complete Key Meditation One: "Grounding," and Key Meditation Two: "White Light," found on pages 20 and 22.

The Healing Room Meditation

1. Take several deep breaths until you feel relaxed.

2. Focus on your third eye and visualize a white spinning disc.

3. The disc grows larger and larger; when full size, step through the center.

4. You find yourself in a white corridor.

5. In front of you are three steps and a white door at the top.

6. Walk forward, climb three steps, open the door, and go inside.

7. You have entered a large white room.

8. The walls are lined with shelves from floor to ceiling with everything to make you feel better and heal you, such as medicines, herbs, books, and music.

9. There are large wicker baskets on your left.

10. You scoop up a handful of petals from a wicker basket on the floor and breathe in the aroma.

11. Then let the petals fall back through your fingertips into the basket.

12. On some of the shelves are brightly colored bottles.

13. Whichever color you are drawn to, take the bottle from the shelf, take off the lid, and smell or taste what is inside.

14. When you have finished, put the bottle back.

15. The back wall of the room is made up of a fine blue mist.

16. Walk into the mist and feel it enter the front of you and sweep right through you, turning you royal blue, inside and out.

17. As you step out of the mist, feel it draw itself out of your back.

18. The wall to your left hand side is made of natural rock and you hear the sound of water running down the rocks as a gentle waterfall.

19. A pool is gathering at the foot of the waterfall.

20. You step toward the pool and put your bare feet in the water.

21. Visualize two small openings in the soles of your feet, drawing the water up into your body.

22. The water rises up your body to the top of your head.

23. When you are full, allow the water to drain back out through your feet.

24. Step out of the pool and close the openings in the soles of your feet.

25. Continue to walk further into the room, and then turn a corner.

26. In front of you is a huge stained glass window through which the sunlight is pouring, lighting up the room with pure shafts of color.

27. Under the window is a large carved chair.

28. Walk over and sit in the chair.

29. It is perfectly contoured to your body and you sit comfortably, stretching out your arms on the armrests.

30. You feel the sunlight soaking into the top of your head, shoulders, forearms, legs, and then the whole of your body.

31. You feel the sunshine soaking into you skin and muscles and bone structure and energizing the very core of you.

32. When you are energized, get up out of the chair and make your way back.

33. Turn the corner toward the blue mist passing the waterfall (on your right).

34. Once again walk through the blue mist.

35. Make your way back through the room toward the door.

36. Stop at the door and look back at the room.

37. You can come to your own healing room whenever you feel you need to.

38. You can add to the shelves anything personal that you use to make yourself feel better physically, mentally, or emotionally.

39. Now go through the door and leave the room.

40. Come back down the steps and walk back along the path.

41. Come back into your body. When you are ready open your eyes.

The Visiting Room Meditation

In this meditation you travel to visit a healer. This can be a very effective meditation if you have a strong belief in a particular healer, someone who has actually treated you in the past, or a well-known healer who you have read about or heard about. If you have a photograph or picture, focus on this in preparation for your "visit."

This meditation is most effective if you are lying down.

1. Close your eyes, relax, and take your focus to your third eye.

2. Visualize a white spinning disk, growing larger and larger.

3. When it is large enough, step through the center.

4. Visualize you are on your way to your chosen healer's practice.

5. You arrive at the door of their surgery.

6. You enter and make your way to the waiting room.

7. You wait until you are called into the treatment room.

8. Visualize the room as you walk in and greet the healer.

9. You lay on the couch and the healer begins the treatment.

10. Allow yourself to relax and you will feel energies at work.

11. When you feel the healing has finished, *thank the healer.*

12. Make your way out of the building.

13. Return through the light of your third eye.

14. Blend in with your body.

Note: If, during this meditation, you fall asleep while you are having the treatment, don't worry because you won't do yourself any damage. As soon as you wake up, perform Key Meditation One: "Grounding." If you regularly practice this meditation you will feel something different happening each time, as the healing changes according to your needs.

Part Three

SPIRITUAL
MEDITATION

Psychic
Development

11

Everyone is naturally psychic and we all have psychic experiences every day—a "gut feeling," a premonition, or a feeling of "déjà vu." We all read the thoughts of others to some degree, whether we're aware of it or not (have you ever said to yourself, "I knew he was going to say that!"?). Many people experience occasional out-of-body sensations and give some form of healing to themselves.

If you think back to when you were a child, you may remember knowing certain things without being told. You may have felt spirit people around you, or you may have had incredible, vivid dreams. Psychic ability springs from our natural instincts and it is a natural extension of our intuition. If we choose to disregard our natural intuition it will remain dormant, but if we listen and pay attention to it, our lives can really open up.

Psychic information comes from our physical senses of touch, hearing, sight, smell, and taste. These senses not only experience the physical or "solid" world around us, but they can work together to become a *sixth sense* or a *psychic sense*. When we pick up information psychically, we experience it in a multi-sensory manner, because we see, hear, feel, smell, and taste beyond what is immediately around us. Our senses work by reading energies, including those that surround people and those that create atmospheres. This psychism can also include "seeing" future happenings.

To develop psychically the happier and more relaxed you are, the faster you will progress in your psychic development. Meditation is an intrinsic part of refining your psychic skills, and it can help you lift your vibration, and the higher your vibration the happier you feel.

Clairsentience

Clairsentience, or "clear feeling," is the sense that nearly all of us are aware of. It can range from a gut feeling, a sense of danger, a strong sensation, or just *knowing* something. It is the impression you make when you meet someone for the first time, and the common feeling of walking into a room and feeling uneasy. When you develop this sense you can expand this so that you can pick up on something that is wrong, sometimes in great detail. Clairsentience is more common in emotionally based people than in logical people, and more common among women and children than among men.

The following isn't so much a meditation as a way of opening yourself to the atmospheres that your and other people's energies create:

Focus on feeling what the energy is like around you, and wherever you are try to feel the energy or atmosphere of the place. Try to sense the different energy in different places, such as shops, different streets, the doctor's surgery or the various rooms of your home. Do the same in natural surroundings such as the countryside, or your garden, in a park, in woodland, or by the sea. This is easy to practice, so try and sense the energy of where you are.

Examine the effect that nature has by sensing what the energy is like in early morning, at midday, in the late afternoon, at dusk or at night. Let yourself be aware of the feelings that different types of music generate. Tune into the feeling that various people emit or those that animals give you. Finally gauge the feelings that your thoughts evoke.

Clairvoyance

Clairvoyance is French for "clear seeing," and this ability goes a step further than just seeing the solid world around us. It is a matter of receiving information the mind's eye or "the third eye" in the form of images or symbols that represent situations and feelings. There are some clairvoyants who see images of animals from the spirit world or the auras around living things. Some people see things exactly as they are, while others see things in the form of symbols. Many clairvoyants use both techniques. A typical symbol a clairvoyant might see is a ring when someone is getting engaged, or a crib when a baby is coming, and so forth. These are well-known as symbols. Other clairvoyant images, such as archetypes, need interpretation. Archetypes are original and ancient symbols that our ancestors would understand. An example would be a jester, which would mean fun and laughter or entertainment. Another would be that of a wise old woman, symbolizing ancient knowledge. A sword would predict trouble or fighting. The theory is that some part of our memory is inherited from our ancestors; this is known as "ancestral memory," and it transcends space and time. Therefore, these images and archetypes are understood and recognized universally.

Symbols can also be very personal to each individual as they come from each person's subconscious mind. You could ask someone how he or she is feeling and then clairvoyantly "see" an image of your bed. You know that it is daytime and that the only time you find yourself in bed during the day is when you are ill. Then the person tells you he or she has been ill. You might meet someone new and suddenly get a passing flash of an image of someone else, and this tells you that the new person is like the one whose image you picked up. You may see objects or situations in your life that show you something in theirs, such as a part of your house, and then discover that they are altering the same part in their own house.

A particular symbol can mean something different to each person. For instance, for one person a bar of chocolate represents something that they have given up eating, but someone else would see it as a source of energy or a source of pleasure. Symbols are not fixed with one meaning, so you have to go with what you feel with each image.

The following is a light meditation that will help you to develop your clairvoyance.

1. Create a scene you enjoy such as a lovely sandy beach, a woodland, or country walk.

2. Try to focus on seeing as much detail as possible, including the leaves on the trees, blades of grass, and grains of sand.

3. Then open up your other senses and imagine what sounds you would hear, and imagine the natural elements that you would feel, such as warm sun or a cool breeze.

4. Touch things and imagine their texture.

5. Ask yourself: What smells and tastes would you find there?

6. Focus on the point between your eyebrows where your "third eye" is situated.

7. Visualize a closed camera shutter and open it.

8. Inside is another closed camera shutter; open this one as well.

9. Yet again there is another shutter inside; keep opening shutters, layer after layer.

(You can use the image of a flower instead if you like, and in this case, you open the petals bit by bit.)

If you practice this meditation, you will strengthen your ability to use clairvoyance accurately and see images clearer.

Clairaudience

Our sense of clairaudience, or "clear hearing," involves hearing impressions of sounds, words, voices, or music that are not heard by normal hearing; the sounds will seem to originate in your head, or to one side of your head and slightly behind one ear. Sometimes you will get a clairvoyant image, such as an initial letter, at the same time that you experience clairaudience.

The main proof you are experiencing clairaudience is when you are hearing words that you would not normally use or that you do not know. You might hear these in your own voice or less commonly in the voice of another person. Clairaudient messages can come from the telepathic thoughts of others, where you may actually "hear" what the other person is thinking, although you will usually pick up fragments of sentences. It can also come from people who are now in the spirit world and who want to pass on messages, or it can come from a spirit guide. This is part of mediumship, which is also called channeling.

With clairaudience we will hear some things clearly, but at other times, the sounds will be fuzzy and unclear, like being slightly off channel when tuning into a radio station. All that may be picked up is a general sound of a word or initial. You may be hearing the name Sheryl but only actually hear the "sh" sound, or a guide might be passing on the name Jamie and all you hear is the "ee" sound. Clairaudience is a case of tuning into the right frequencies. Both physical sound and clairaudient sound vibrates at certain rates so it is achieved by widening our range of certain frequencies.

This light meditation will help you to make a start on clairaudience or improve on the gift you already have:

1. Focus on conjuring natural sounds in your head, such as wind through the trees, rain on the window, or a waterfall.

2. Concentrate on the sound of a crowded room, a train station, and on different voices.

3. Focus on the sounds of music, various instruments, individual singers, and choirs.

4. Tune into more subtle sounds, like a fire burning, a clock ticking, or the sound of your breath.

A Special Meditation for Clairaudience

1. Imagine a golden light around your head and ears.

2. Now imagine that you have a radio tuner inside your head.

3. When you tune it in to certain stations, you can pick up different frequencies.

4. There is a main station connecting you to your psychic abilities, so take a few moments to tune into that station; let your hearing begin to subtly change and expand.

5. Now there are further channels, one to connect you with the world of animals and plants, another for telepathy with other people, one for messages from people in the spirit world, and one for spirit guides who can help and teach you.

6. Choose a channel and try to sense a fine sound.

7. Leave yourself open to any sounds that you may hear.

8. When you have finished, move the channel finder to a lower frequency and let your hearing adjust to normal hearing.

Try and avoid noisy, bustling places right after this meditation.

Clairalience and Clairambience

Clairalience means "clear smelling," and clairambience denotes "clear tasting." This may sound far-fetched, but smelling things that aren't there is an extremely common form of psychic ability. For example, you smell smoke, yet there is no fire or anybody around you smoking. These impressions are usually connected to the spirit world, often indicating that a spirit is near. These smells can vary from scents of flowers, perfumes, cigarette smoke, to smells of baking or tastes of food or certain drinks. Sometimes the past lingers, so that you enter a building and smell what used to be there, such as a smell of animals that used to be kept there. Alternatively, you may smell hay or manure.

Tastes can include sweet tastes, such as sugar, and other foods or drinks. Taste sensations of damp or freshness from way back in the past can linger around a building. A musty smell might be a symbol of the age of a building and of the passage of time, while freshness indicates the future.

Sometimes when you are searching your head for a word of advice for someone, instead of words you may be given smells or tastes that have a symbolic meaning, such as "wake up and smell the coffee." A smell or taste will jog your memory or bring a proverb to mind.

Developing Your Psychic Smell and Taste Senses

Be aware of different smells and tastes everywhere you go, such as inside shops, markets, other people's homes, the street, in a town or city center, around different people, or out of doors. See if you can detect any smells that do not belong or do not seem to be coming from anything physical. Then focus on the smells of objects such as things made of wood, metal, plastic, or liquid. Do clothes smell different to the upholstery of your furniture? When you are away from these places and objects try to imagine their smells. Focus on the way that food and drinks taste and remember the taste after you have finished eating or drinking. Can you conjure up the taste of your favorite food? Perhaps bitter tastes, sweet tastes different textures of food.

Bring certain smells and tastes to mind and see who or what you relate them to, such as whom a certain scent reminds you of. Write these down and familiarize these symbols, as this will help your use of psychic symbols.

Claircognition

Claircognition is "clear knowing." Often we are able to receive knowledge and information through our extra-senses, such as information from people who have lived in the past or from creative theories and books. On the astral levels, there are circuits of information that we can all tap into, and all you normally need is enthusiasm and a strong urge to do so. Creative people such as artists, writers, musicians, all tap into circuits that are forms of thought and energy from past creative souls. Sometimes this knowledge feels the same as inspiration. Knowledge can also come through via our guides and spirit helpers.

Telepathy

The phone rings and you know who's on the other end of the line before you answer is telepathy, as is you and another person having the same idea at the same moment. This is not so much a psychic power but a *telepathic* link. Thoughts possess their own energy, which can travel over great distances in an instant. The stronger the feelings behind the thought the more impact it will have. If someone is thinking of you with feelings of devoted love, anger, passion or hatred you may feel it.

We are all telepathic to some degree, receiving and transmitting information most of the time without being aware of it. Some of us are better at transmitting while others are successful receivers. The thoughts you receive telepathically will often be a mixture of images, feelings or words or phrases that may link together to make sense or they may be random bits and pieces.

Strengthening Your Telepathic Skills

Take a willing friend or someone you know well and sit opposite them. Tell them to relax and shut your eyes. Visualize that you are inside their head and looking out of their eyes. See what impressions, images, feelings, and body sensations you may get. Tell the other person of anything that you receive. If you feel resistance and cannot engage with them to look out of their eyes do not persist. Your partner has put up a block and you will not be able to overcome this. Instead visualize yourself standing behind the person within their energy field. Tell them what you are receiving, but don't be discouraged if you are wrong while you're still new to this.

This exercise will show how to transmit thoughts. Enlist the help of a friend and then take a few minutes to visualize them in a simple situation that can evoke feelings, such as walking in an icy wind, standing by a warm fire, floating in water, climbing a mountain, or flying. Ask them how they feel to see if they have received the sensations from you. Keep experimenting and you will soon improve.

Note: Be careful of using telepathy to send thoughts to hurt or upset someone, as doing so only lowers your own psychic vibration and you leave yourself open to unpleasant energies.

Remote Viewing

Remote viewing or astral projection is a stronger form of telepathy. It is taking your mind to a distant place and being able to see it or to "be there," or to know what is happening there. It is believed we can also travel in time as well as distance and see events that happened a long time ago or even view parts of future events.

Many of us can astrally project or travel to various locations on earth, or some people can apparently explore other planets and dimensions. Some people believe that we leave our bodies most nights when we are in the deepest part of our sleep, and travel around our planet or beyond. However, when you learn to view by remote means, it is best to begin by using a place that is familiar to you, and to move on to unfamiliar locations later. This process will take perseverance as it takes time to master.

Strengthening Your Remote Viewing Skills

Work with a friend whose home you are familiar with and ask them to go into their bedroom or into some other room where they are unlikely to be disturbed. Ask your friend to move or set up some items around the room or on the floor. Visualize yourself going into house, entering by the main door and making your way to their room. As you go along, try to see with as much detail of the house, just as if you were physically there. When you reach the experimental room, try and see it as you remember it from previous visits, then scan for impressions of the things that your friend has placed there. Check with your friend to see how accurate you are. After you have had some practice at this ask your friend to place an object in a box or container and see if you can find it, describe it, and say what is inside.

Meditation
for Spiritual
Connection

12

The spirit world exists on a higher level than ours, and the energy of the spirit world has a faster vibration than ours. When spirit beings communicate with us, they slow their vibration down, and in our turn, we need to speed ours up so our energies can match and meet on the same level. To speed up your vibration so that you can receive information and messages is very simple. The calmer and happier you are the higher your energy vibration lifts. You need to open your energy centers or chakras, because these are your psychic and spiritual centers. By grounding, opening up and using white light you can lift your vibration and rid yourself of surplus negative energy.

Opening Your Chakras

Before you begin to open your chakras, please complete Key Meditation One: "Grounding," and Key Meditation Two: "White Light." These meditations will prepare you for following spiritual meditations where you can meet spirit guides, relatives who have passed on, angels, and spirit masters. These meditations will open your chakras or psychic centers.

Root or base chakra

Some people call this the root chakra, others call it the base chakra, and it is located two centimeters forward from the base of your spine. It is the slowest spinning chakra and it creates the color crimson as it spins. Visualize this chakra as a closed red flower head and focus on it opening, then once the petals are fully open, imagine a round clear space in the center of the flower. Then imagine white light spinning in this center.

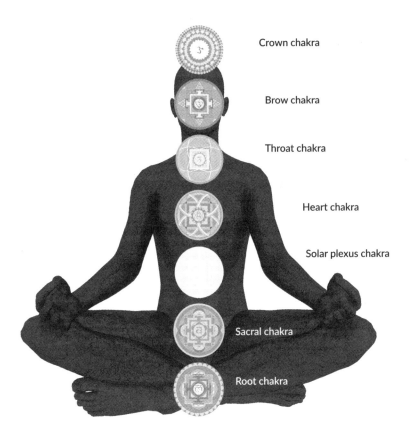

Crown chakra

Brow chakra

Throat chakra

Heart chakra

Solar plexus chakra

Sacral chakra

Root chakra

Sacral chakra

Move up to the center of your abdomen about two inches under your navel. Here is your sacral chakra. This chakra spins slightly faster than the root chakra, creating the color orange. Open the petals of the orange flower head and open the center of the flower head giving you a round clear space. Spin the clear space or center with white light.

Solar plexus chakra

Your solar plexus is situated just slightly above the navel. (Some people feel theirs toward the left of the navel.) This chakra spins faster than the sacral chakra and creates the color yellow. Open the yellow aperture or flower head and center. Spin the clear center with white light.

Heart chakra

Move up to the center of your chest to your heart chakra, which spins at a medium speed creating the color emerald green. Open up your green flower head and clear the center of the flower. Spin the open center with white light.

Throat chakra

Your throat chakra is situated at the lower end of your neck. This spins at a fast rate of vibration and creates a vibrant sky blue. Open up the blue flower head and clear the center allowing it to spin with white light.

Brow chakra or third eye

Your brow chakra or third eye is positioned between and slightly above your eyebrows, and it is colored indigo, which is a dark blue color. Open the flower head and center, clear the center and fill it with white light, which you then spin.

Crown chakra

Now move to the crown of your head and your crown or seventh chakra. This chakra is either visualized as white or pale lilac. Open the petals then the flower center and clear it and then fill it with white light, which you then spin.

Using a Light Body

A very effective way to connect to the spirit world is to wear what is called a "light body." The strongest of these are the shamanic light bodies of power animals, such as an eagle, snow owl, hawk, brown bear or polar bear, wolf, raven, or crow. If you don't know which type to use, go back to chapter 9 and work with different power animal meditations until you make a connection.

Once you have opened up your centers, visualize yourself receiving a beautiful crystal robe in the shape of a bird or animal. If you have decided to use an eagle, visualize the feathers as crystal, or if using an animal, see the fur as crystal fibers. If you decide to use an eagle, visualize the crystal head of the eagle sitting over your head, and for a couple of seconds focus on looking out of the eyes of the eagle and imagine you are this strong, alert, high flying bird. Your arms become the wings and the back of the bird becomes your back. Your legs and feet become that of the eagle and the bird's underbody closes around the front of your body. You become aware that you have millions of feathers, which will be enough for all the frequencies available for you to tune into. Sweep light from the bottom of your feet to the top of your head, lifting and lighting the feathers.

Now you can ask to work with your highest guides, which are of absolute light. Ask them three times to come and work with you. Ask for the room's energies to be cleared and the will of God, the Great Spirit, the Universe, or the Source to be done.

Energy Protection

This meditation will prevent you from feeling super sensitive to atmospheres and to the negative emotions of others. An effective energy protection is to use colored cloaks. Powerful healing and protecting colors to use are gold, silver, or the three universal healing colors of blue, orange, or green.

1. First, choose the color you feel you like or need.

2. Feel a cloak in your chosen color come down from above in a tube of light, until it falls over your shoulders and fastens at the base of your neck over your throat center.

3. Close the cloak over your body chakras and bring a large hood up over your head with the front falling over your third eye.

4. Keep putting on cloaks one atop the other, until you feel there is a layer of protection around you.

5. It is useful to make the final cloak brown or to turn the surface brown, as this is a good color for mental clarity and grounding.

Other forms of protection are to imagine shamanic drums sitting over the solar plexus and abdomen. This form of protection bounces negative energy straight back to those who are sending it. Negative energy includes insults, anger, aggression, criticism, and abuse. You can visualize a mirror over your solar plexus or imagine wearing a full-mirrored suit of armor, complete with helmet, visor, body suit, gloves, and boots if venturing into very difficult situations. Negative energy thrown at you will bounce back to its source very quickly, and this can even make people aware of how badly they are behaving. It's worth remembering that if you don't take the bait when these people make negative remarks, the negative energy immediately returns to the sender.

The Universal Healing Plane

This allows you to give healing to yourself and others. Start by completing Key Meditation Three: "Spinning Disc," on page 24.

1.   In front of you is a white stairway leading upward.

2. You climb up a set of thirty steps and cross a landing.

3. Across the landing is a short set of five stairs. You climb up them.

4. Across the landing is a set of seven stairs. You climb up the last seven stairs.

5. At the top is a doorway, leading into a large crystal hall.

6. You walk in and make your way through the hall.

7. There are large crystal precipices that project over a pure water stream.

8. You sit on the edge and your feet dip into the cool running water.

9. A strong white light flows down through the crown of your head, through your body, and pushes any negative energy out of your feet.

10. Watch the negativity float away down the stream.

11. When you are ready, stand and make your way back to the entrance.

12. There is now a straight stairway leading down.

13. Return to ground level and the hallway.

14. Leave the house and make your way back through the garden.

15. Then return through your third eye.

16. When you are ready, open your eyes.

The Closing Sequence

At the end of a meditation or spiritual working session it is important to close down your chakras or you will be leaving yourself too open and will feel vulnerable to everyone's negative energy.

Take your attention to your crown chakra, dim the light, and slow down the spinning. Close the open center of the chakra petals. Then follow the same sequence moving down to your third eye, then throat, then heart, solar plexus, sacral or abdomen chakra, then root or base chakra. Visualize the "light body" lifting from your shoulders, and send it up into the shaft of white light. You can simply open your eyes or you can put on some energy protection.

Meditation and Religion

13

Many religions encourage people to meditate for various purposes; for example, if you were to go into a Catholic retreat, you might be encouraged you to meditate on your own life and on Christian images, or recite the rosary, which is a form meditation.

Following is a brief overview of some well-known religions, along with a selection of their meditations.

Buddhism

Buddhism comes from the teachings of the Lord Buddha, and the word *Buddha* comes from Sanskrit and means "awakening." The main aim of Buddhism is to achieve spiritual enlightenment, thus enabling the followers to live a happier life. Unlike other religions, Buddhism deals with guidance through teaching, not with upholding traditions or revelations of truth. There are three parts to Buddhism known as "The Three Jewels," and these are the *Buddha*, *Dharma*, and *Sangha*.

The Buddha was the man who discovered and taught the path to enlightenment and happiness. He is seen as mortal so he proves that it is possible for all human beings to achieve enlightenment, though it may take many lifetimes.

The Dharma means "as it is" or "what is" and it refers to the teachings of Buddha. The Dharma includes The Four Noble Truths;The Eightfold Path; *dukkha*, which means inevitable suffering; *samsara*, which is the cycle of birth, life, death and rebirth; *anicca*, which shows that nothing lasts forever; and lastly karma, which is the chain of cause and effect.

Every moment that your mind is free of greed, hate or delusion, the Buddhists believe a force develops called *parami*, which is a pure force of energy that builds within your mind. When you have a great accumulation of pure force then the results are many kinds of happiness. There are two kinds of *parami*, or the purity of mind, and this is shown in two ways: the purity of actions and the purity of wisdom.

Meditation is central to Buddhism, so there are many different kinds of meditation for a variety of purposes. Following is a lovely one that is designed to encourage you to develop a pleasing and friendly attitude.

The Metta Bhavana

1. Find a quiet place to sit and relax and close your eyes.

2. Follow your breaths counting beats for how long you can breath out for and how long you can breath in.

3. Do this for a few minutes if you can.

4. Think of good positive feelings that you have for yourself, focusing on pleasant things about yourself by silently saying such things as "I am happy" or "I am well." Alternatively, dwell on a memory of a time when you felt really happy, or wish yourself happiness and let the feeling grow.

5. Then think of someone you know in your life, such as a good friend.

6. Picture them really happy and wish them happiness.

7. Next choose a person that you do not know very well, whom you have no strong like or dislike for, such as a person you see in passing every day on the train or at work. Picture them happy and wish them happiness.

8. Next, choose someone you do not like at all, someone who works against you or who has hurt or upset you in some way.

9. Try to see past their bad points and realize that they just want to be happy.

10. Picture them happy and wish them happiness.

11. Now picture the friend, the neutral person, the enemy, and yourself all feeling the same good feelings, and then wish happiness to all four of you.

12. Now widen your scope and think of others around you; picture them and wish them happiness.

13. Then look beyond to those who live in your area, in your town; then your province; then your country.

14. Think of all the people who live there and feel and wish them well.

15. Wish them the same happiness that you wish yourself.

16. Then think of everyone in the world and all living creatures and picture them happy and wish them happiness.

Mantras

Mantra comes from the Sanskrit word *mantrana*, which means "suggestion" or "advice." Mantras are words or phrases whose sound vibrations have a strong impact on the person saying them and also on those who hear them. Each word has a sound pattern that reaches the mind with its meaning and is also a trigger for the emotions. They are regarded as power words and are used as a focus in Buddhist meditation. One such mantra is *Om mani padme hum*, which means "Jewel in the lotus of the heart." It is used to open up the heart center, allowing you to give love and kindness as well as accept it from others. As a meditation, you sit quietly and repeat a mantra either in your mind or out loud, focusing on the words and the sounds that they make. They are meant to be repeated many times, and for several minutes, preferably every day.

Zen

In approximately AD 475, a Buddhist teacher named Bodhidharma took Buddhist teachings to China. There the teachings spread, blended with Taoism, and became the Ch'an School of Buddhism. Seven hundred years later, Ch'an Buddhism went to Japan where it became known as Zen Buddhism. It is the base of the martial arts of karate, and also of archery and swordsmanship. Many people take up Zen meditation because it improves concentration in sports and athletics as well as academic study. The following is one form of Zen meditation.

Zazen

This is the predominant method of Zen meditation; it means "sitting." Zazen uses breathing as the main focus to clear the mind, so you breathe in and out deeply, focusing on the rise and fall of the abdomen, while observing the cool inhalation of air and the exhalation of warm air. The practitioner pays attention to the way the nostril feels, to the air tracts, and to the head, and what happens to these with each intake of breath.

Tao

Tao focuses on developing a sense of unity of mind, body, and spirit. When this unity is achieved we are able to achieve what we want and do good for ourselves and for others. Tao teaches us not to look at life with our rational mind so much, but to experience life more like an adventure and to follow what we are fascinated by. In a way, you look at life as if it is a fairy tale, letting go of agendas, and just experiencing the ride. In Taoist beliefs, happiness comes in phases or in cycles: we go through good times, we go through bad times, and then we go through good times again. The phase we are presently in is often followed by its opposite; a hectic social phase may be followed by a phase of quiet where we become quite lonely; then the hectic social life picks up again.

Tao is a Chinese philosophy, the main part of which is that you aim to truly appreciate *being* here, in the moment, and enjoying life. Without joy there is not much point in being here! Tao is not so much a religion as a way of being. Translated, the word *Tao* means "the way."

In Tao everything is made up of, or works through, two opposite forces—yin and yang. Yin and yang are in every aspect of life and everything is made up of these two opposites. Yin is passive, feminine, cool, and slow. Yang is energetic, masculine, hot, and fast.

Some examples are:

- Sun is yang, moon is yin.
- Light is yang, dark is yin.
- Summer is yang, winter is yin.
- Boy is yang, girl is yin.
- Busy is yang, quiet is yin.
- Success is yang, failure is yin.

Yin and yang are related to the five elemental forces that make up the core of our world. These five elemental forces are water, wood, fire, earth, and metal.

Mindfulness Meditation

1. Sit quietly and focus on your breathing.

2. No matter what kind of thought comes into your mind, say to yourself, "That may be an important issue in my life, but right now is not the time to think about it. Right now I am meditating."

3. Return your focus to your breathing, and find yourself at peace with the here and now.

Try another practical guide in the
ORION PLAIN AND SIMPLE series

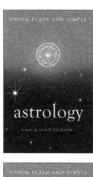

ORION PLAIN AND SIMPLE

astrology

CASS & JANIE JACKSON

ORION PLAIN AND SIMPLE

totem animals

CELIA M GUNN

ORION PLAIN AND SIMPLE

runes

KIM FARNELL

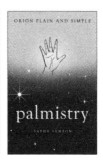

ORION PLAIN AND SIMPLE

palmistry

SASHA FENTON

ORION PLAIN AND SIMPLE

body reading

SASHA FENTON

ORION PLAIN AND SIMPLE

numerology

ANNE CHRISTIE

ORION PLAIN AND SIMPLE

chinese astrology

JONATHAN DEE

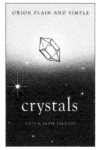

ORION PLAIN AND SIMPLE

crystals

CASS & JANIE JACKSON

ORION PLAIN AND SIMPLE

reincarnation

EDES & CASS GODLY

ORION PLAIN AND SIMPLE

angels

BELUGA GREENAWAY

ORION PLAIN AND SIMPLE

wicca

LEANNA GREENAWAY

ORION PLAIN AND SIMPLE

herbs

MARLENE HOUGHTON

ORION PLAIN AND SIMPLE

i ching

KIM FARNELL

ORION PLAIN AND SIMPLE

flower essences

LINDA PERRY

OG